❤Thank you for purchasing this book!

· I hope it's already catching your attention and that you're finding something useful or interesting between these pages.

✍If you have a free minute, I'd be happy to read your opinion on Amazon: even a short review is a big help for me and other readers like you!

· Want a gift? Scan the QR code below to download a very funny book for free , designed to make you smile after this reading!

· It's available in 5 languages: Italian, English, French, German and Spanish.

· By subscribing, you'll also receive updates about upcoming books and special content dedicated to you.

· Thanks again for your support! · I can't wait to meet you in my next book!

https://xcapire.it/regalo/

THE STORY OF

SANTA CLAUS

FROM MYRA TO THE NORTH POLE

Story of a Turkish Bishop
Who Became the Symbol of Christmas

INTRODUCTION

In the heart of ancient Anatolia, among the dusty streets of a city called Myra, an extraordinary story begins that will cross continents and centuries, transforming itself like a river that, starting from a small spring, expands until it becomes a mighty watercourse. It is the story of a man whose original name, Nikolaos, still resonates today in hundreds of different languages, even if few would recognize in that young bishop with olive skin and a dark cloak the cheerful character dressed in red that every child in the modern world knows as Santa Claus.

As the sun sets over the Mediterranean, turning the domes of Myra's churches gold, we can almost see young Nicholas walking the streets of his hometown, unaware that his charitable deeds would spark one of the most extraordinary cultural transformations in human history. How did a third-century saint in what is now Turkey become the embodiment of Christmas joy? How did his bishop's robe and pastoral staff transform into a shiny red jacket trimmed with white fur and a sack full of toys?

The answer to these questions takes us on a fascinating journey through the ages, where the paths of history intertwine with those of legend, where reality merges with fantasy, and where each culture has added its own piece to an increasingly rich and complex mosaic. It is a journey that will lead us from the sunny coasts of the Mediterranean to the foggy medieval cities of Northern Europe, from the lively streets of nineteenth-century New York to the frozen expanses of the North Pole.

On this journey we will meet Venetian merchants who steal sacred relics in the dead of night, poets who write verses destined to change the Christmas imagination forever, and artists who with their brushes will shape the dreams of millions of children. We will see how ancient pagan legends have merged with Christian tradition, how the industrial revolution has transformed a saint into a commercial icon, and how, despite all these changes, the original message of generosity and love has remained surprisingly intact.

But this is not just the story of a character who has evolved over time. It is also the story of how human societies create and transform their symbols, how traditions travel and adapt, how cultures influence each other in often unpredictable ways. It is a testimony to how a single act of kindness can generate ripples that propagate through the centuries, touching the lives of billions of people.

As you leaf through these pages, you will discover that the true magic of this story lies not in the supernatural powers attributed to Santa Claus, but in humanity's ability to create meaning and beauty across generations. You will see how each era and each people have contributed to shaping this figure, adding details, modifying traditions, creating new rituals, until building something that is far more than the sum of its parts.

In an age when the world seems increasingly divided, the story of how a Turkish bishop became a universal symbol of joy and generosity reminds us that cultural differences can be bridges rather than barriers. It shows us how the most beautiful and enduring traditions are often those that arise from the encounter between different traditions, from the fusion of seemingly incompatible elements, from the human capacity to continually reinvent and reinterpret its own cultural heritage.

This book is an invitation to look beneath the glittering surface of modern Christmas to discover the deep roots of one of the most beloved figures in tradition. It is a journey that will lead us to understand not only who Saint Nicholas was and how he became Santa Claus, but also something deeper about ourselves and how we create and transmit meaning across generations.

So prepare yourselves for an extraordinary journey, where history intertwines with legend, where faith mixes with fantasy, and where you will discover that the true magic of Christmas lies not in material gifts, but in the human capacity to create stories that unite people of every culture, age and creed in a single, great narrative of hope and generosity.

PROLOGUE: THE MYSTERY OF THE RED DRESS

Snow falls silently in Times Square on this Christmas Eve in 1931. Neon lights reflect off the white flakes, creating a kaleidoscope of color that dances in the chilly New York air. Amid the crowds of people busy with last-minute Christmas shopping, an artist named Haddon Sundblom is returning to his studio, clutching a folder full of sketches. He has just finished a meeting with Coca-Cola executives, and his mind is racing. He has been commissioned to do something seemingly simple: paint Santa Claus for an advertising campaign. Yet as he climbs the stairs to his studio, Sundblom knows there is something deeper to this assignment.

He turns on the lamp on his desk and starts leafing through old books and illustrations. On the pages yellowed by time, he finds different representations of Santa Claus: some show him tall and thin, others short and corpulent. In some images he wears a green cape, in others a brown fur coat. How is it possible that such an iconic character has had so many different incarnations? And why has red become his signature color?

The question bounces around in the artist's mind as he watches children playing in the snow from his studio window. A century earlier, in that very same city, another artist, Thomas Nast, had given his interpretation of Santa Claus. And even before that, poets and writers had helped shape the image of this mysterious character. But where did this figure really come from? What story was hidden behind that jovial face and that white beard?

In a corner of his study, Sundblom notices an old book on the history of Byzantine art. He opens it absentmindedly and stops at an illustration that catches his eye: it is the portrait of a bishop who lived in the third century in a city called Myra, in modern-day Turkey. The man in the image is wearing bishop's vestments and has a kind look. The caption reads: "Saint Nicholas of Myra." Something about that look reminds him strangely of the expression he is trying to capture for his Santa Claus.

It is extraordinary to think how a bishop who lived almost two thousand years ago in a distant land became the universal symbol of Christmas. How did his bishop's cloak become the characteristic red dress we all know today? And why did this Mediterranean saint end up being associated with the cold North Pole?

To answer these questions we will take a journey through time and space, a journey that crosses continents and cultures, that intertwines history and legend, faith and folklore. It is a story that speaks of how traditions evolve and transform, how stories travel and adapt to new contexts, how symbols acquire new meanings while maintaining their deepest essence intact.

As Sundblom begins to sketch his Santa Claus, he can't help but think of all the people who have helped create this figure over the centuries. Venetian merchants who stole holy relics, Dutch sailors who brought their traditions to the New World, poets who gave wings to their imaginations, artists who gave shape to children's dreams.

The red that he is about to spread on his canvas is not only the color of a dress, but the common thread of a thousand-year-old story. It is the color of the bishop's robes of Saint Nicholas, the color of the fire that warmed homes on cold nights in Northern Europe, the color that has come to symbolize the joy and magic of Christmas throughout the world.

Outside the window, snow continues to fall on New York. Somewhere in the city, a child is probably writing his letter to Santa Claus, unaware that the figure he is addressing is the result of centuries of cultural evolution, of encounters between different civilizations, of transformations and adaptations. He does not know that behind that red dress lies a story that spans continents and centuries, a story that speaks of generosity, of miracles, of hope.

It is a story that begins in a coastal city of ancient Anatolia, where a young bishop performed acts of charity that would be remembered for centuries. A story that takes us through the foggy medieval cities of Northern Europe, where Christian legends merged with ancient pagan traditions. A story that crosses the Atlantic with Dutch immigrants, that transforms into the streets of New York, and that eventually reaches every corner of the world.

But it is also a story that tells us about how human societies create and transform their own symbols, how traditions adapt to cultural and social changes, how a single character can take on different meanings for different people, while keeping intact its fundamental message of generosity and hope.

As Sundblom applies the first red brushstrokes to his canvas, he is contributing, perhaps without knowing it, to the last chapter of this extraordinary transformation. His Santa Claus, with his red suit and cheerful face, will become the definitive image of this character for future generations. But behind that image lies a much older and deeper story, a story that is worth telling.

In the pages that follow, we will retrace this extraordinary journey. We will discover how a Turkish bishop became the symbol of Christmas, how his bishop's cloak was transformed into the characteristic red dress, and how his story crossed centuries and continents to become one of the most beloved narratives in the world. It is a journey that will take us from Myra to the North Pole, through real and imaginary lands, through history and legend, to discover how one of the most powerful and universal symbols of our culture was born.

Chapter 1: The Origins - Saint Nicholas of Myra

Third Century Turkey: A Meeting Place of Cultures

The salty Mediterranean air mingled with the scents of exotic spices wafting from Myra's harbor, while the setting sun painted the city's ancient walls gold. It was 270 AD, and this coastal city in Anatolia was more than just a dot on the map of the Roman Empire: it was a crossroads of cultures, a place where East and West merged in a kaleidoscope of languages, traditions and beliefs.

In the narrow streets of the port, Greek merchants bargained with Syrian traders, while Egyptian sailors unloaded amphorae of wine next to caravans from Persia. Lycia, the region of which Myra was the capital, had already seen the domination of several civilizations: from the Persians to the Greeks, up to the Romans. Each domination had left its mark, creating a unique cultural mosaic.

An ancient writing of the time, found on a papyrus preserved in the library of Alexandria, describes Myra as "a city where the gods of a thousand lands meet in the prayers of sailors and merchants". In fact, temples dedicated to Greek and Roman deities stood next to sanctuaries of oriental cults, while the first Christian communities met discreetly in private homes and catacombs.

Daily life in Myra was a constant cultural exchange. Chinese silks, Indian spices, Egyptian grains, and Greek wines could be found in the markets. Women wore Persian jewelry and Syrian fabrics, while men discussed Greek philosophy and Roman law in the public baths.

The predominant language was Greek, but Latin, Aramaic, Coptic, and Persian could be heard in the streets.

An inscription found on a column in the port reads: "Here come ships from every known land, bringing not only goods, but also stories and gods." This multiculturalism was not without tensions: the Roman authorities tried to maintain order in a city where different, often conflicting, religions and customs coexisted.

Christianity, still a minority religion and sometimes persecuted, was however putting down deep roots in this borderland. The Christian communities of Myra were particularly active in social matters, assisting the poor and sailors in difficulty. This characteristic would have a fundamental influence on the figure of Saint Nicholas and on his future role as protector of the needy.

The dwellings of Myra reflected this cultural mix: houses built in the Roman style alternated with buildings that showed Greek and Oriental influences. Archaeologists have unearthed mosaics that testify to this fusion of styles: Roman geometric patterns intertwine with Oriental symbols and hidden early Christian representations.

Myra's geographical position made it a strategic point on trade routes: located on the southern coast of Anatolia, it was a natural harbor protected from the winds and easy to defend. Ships traveling between Rome and the East often stopped here, transforming the city into an important commercial center.

A contemporary document, a commercial letter written on parchment, describes how "the warehouses of Myra overflow with goods from every corner of the empire, and beyond its borders." The city was famous for its grain, which was stored in enormous granaries carved into the rock, which can still be seen today.

Religious life was particularly lively. In addition to pagan temples and nascent Christian churches, the city was also home to Eastern mystery cults. This coexistence of different faiths created a unique environment, where religious ideas contaminated each other. It is no coincidence that one of the most beloved saints of Christianity was born here.

The catacombs of Myra, used both as burial places and as places of worship by the early Christians, preserve frescoes that testify to this cultural fusion: Christian symbols mix with pagan decorative elements, creating a new and unique artistic language.

The city's administration was in the hands of a local council that was supposed to mediate between the different communities. An inscription found in the city forum mentions "the council of wise men of Myra, who govern with justice over people of every language and custom." This ability to manage diversity would have been fundamental to the development of the figure of Saint Nicholas.

The climate of the region favored the cultivation of olives, vines and wheat. The farmers from the hinterland brought their products to the city market, where they mixed with the exotic goods that arrived by sea. This abundance contrasted with the poverty of some segments of the population, creating the social disparity that would push the young Nicola to dedicate his life to helping the needy.

An interesting detail emerges from the archaeological excavations: coins from all over the known world have been found in the streets of Myra, testifying to the intensity of trade. Some of these coins bear religious symbols from different cultures, demonstrating how trade also facilitated the exchange of ideas and beliefs.

It is in this rich and complex context that the young Nicholas was born and raised. The Myra of the third century was the ideal fertile ground for the formation of a figure who would be able to unite elements of different cultures in a universal message of generosity and love for others. His story, which begins in this crossroads of civilizations, would cross centuries and continents, transforming but always keeping alive his original message.

The vestiges of this ancient city, with its theaters, its rock tombs and its granaries dug into the rock, are still visible today in the modern Turkish city of Demre. They are the silent testimony of an era in which cultural differences were not barriers, but bridges to new syntheses and new possibilities. A legacy that the figure of St. Nicholas, and then Santa Claus, would carry with him on his long journey through history.

THE STORY OF YOUNG NICHOLAS: THE CHILD WHO FASTED

Dawn was turning the walls of one of the wealthiest houses in Myra pink, as young Nicholas, fresh from his awakening, knelt for his morning prayer. It was the year 275 AD, and this child of just five years old was already showing signs of an extraordinary devotion that would have perplexed even the oldest members of the local Christian community.

"Little Nicholas refuses breast milk every Wednesday and Friday," writes Methodius, one of the saint's first biographers, in a manuscript preserved in the library of the monastery of Saint Sabbas. "He feeds only once a day, and even then he eats little, as if he already understands the value of fasting." This testimony, legendary as it may seem, offers us a glimpse into the early childhood of the man who would become one of the most venerated saints in Christianity.

Born to Epiphanius and Joanna, a wealthy couple of devout Christians, Nicholas grew up in a privileged environment but no less sensitive to the suffering of others. His parents were known in the city for their generosity toward the poor, a virtue that young Nicholas would not only inherit but elevate to a guiding principle in his life.

An ancient mosaic, discovered during the excavations of the first church in Myra, depicts a scene from his childhood: a dark-haired boy distributing bread to the poor in front of the door of a patrician house. The inscription in ancient Greek reads: "Little Nicholas, fasting to feed others." This image perfectly crystallizes the essence of the future saint: the ability to transform personal deprivation into a gift for others.

His education was entrusted to the best teachers in Myra. A document of the time, a letter written by a merchant to his brother, mentions "the son of Epiphanius, who studies the scriptures with such intensity that even the most learned are amazed". The young Nicholas showed a particular predilection for sacred texts, but did not disdain the study of Greek philosophy and Roman rhetoric, disciplines that would prove useful to him during the years of his episcopate.

But the life of the young Nicholas was not only study and prayer. A particular episode, passed down by oral tradition and then transcribed in the 10th century, tells of how, at the age of seven, he got lost in the market of Myra while following a group of beggars he wanted to help. He was found hours later in one of the catacombs of the city, intent on praying next to the tombs of the first Christian martyrs.

The dramatic turning point in his life came when he was only thirteen years old. A terrible plague epidemic struck Myra, claiming many victims, including his parents. An ancient chronicle preserved in the monastery of Saint Catherine on Mount Sinai describes that period thus: "Young Nicholas, an orphan but not only, became a father to many other orphans, sharing his inheritance with those who had lost everything".

Instead of closing himself in grief, Nicola transformed the tragedy into an opportunity for spiritual growth. A document from the time reports the words of an elder of the community: "The boy fasts not for mortification, but to have more to give to others. His face is always serene, as if he saw something that we cannot see".

His house became a hub for the needy in Myra. The city archives preserve a register of donations from the time that repeatedly mentions "the house of young Nicholas" as a source of aid for widows and orphans. But what most struck his contemporaries was the manner in which he made these donations: always in secret, preferably at night, avoiding any form of public recognition.

A particular aspect of his youth, handed down by multiple sources, concerns his relationship with the sea. Son of a port city, Nicholas spent a lot of time at the port, not so much for commercial interest, but to help the families of sailors in difficulty. A graffito found on a pier in ancient Myra reads: "Here the young Nicholas awaited the return of the ships, praying for the sailors".

His adolescence was marked by long periods of study and prayer, interspersed with increasingly organized and targeted charitable actions. A document from the time describes how he developed a system to identify the neediest families, noting the names and needs of each on wax tablets.

At the age of nineteen, Nicholas undertook a pilgrimage to the Holy Land, a journey that would profoundly affect him. Upon his return, as a contemporary chronicle reports, "his fast had become more severe, but his smile brighter." It was shortly after this journey that the Christian community of Myra began to look to him as a possible future spiritual leader.

His youth ended with an event that foreshadowed his future role as a bishop: during a famine, he organized a relief network involving merchants of different religions, demonstrating that ability to unite different people that would become one of his most distinctive characteristics.

The young fasting Nicholas was destined to become much more than a saint: he would become a universal symbol of generosity and love for others. But in those early years of his life, no one could have imagined that this child with such unusual behaviors would become a central figure in the history of Christianity and, centuries later, the most beloved character by children throughout the world.

THE MIRACLE OF THE THREE SISTERS: THE BIRTH OF A LEGEND

In 4th-century Myra, the dusty streets of the port city told endless stories of merchants, sailors, and families struggling to survive. One in particular would forever mark the life of young Nicholas and give rise to the legend of his extraordinary generosity.

In a small alley not far from the port lived a merchant, once wealthy, fallen from grace after a series of bad investments and storms that had swallowed up his ships loaded with precious goods. The man, now a widower, had three daughters of extraordinary beauty, but the poverty that gripped the family was about to force him to make a heartbreaking choice.

"I can't afford dowries for my daughters," she confided one evening to her old friend Teodoro, as they warmed themselves in front of a brazier in the courtyard. "Without a dowry, no respectable man will ever marry them. The only way out I see is... it's unthinkable, but I have no choice but to send them to the brothel."

The merchant's words reached the ears of the young Nicholas, who in those days had received a large inheritance from his parents, who had died during the epidemic that had struck the city a few years earlier. The chronicles of the time, collected in the manuscript "Praxis de Stratelatis" preserved in the library of the monastery of San Saba in Rome, tell that Nicholas could not sleep for three consecutive nights, tormented by the thought of those young lives on the verge of being ruined.

One night of the new moon, when the streets of Myra were plunged into deep darkness, a bag full of gold coins flew through the open window of the merchant's house. The chronicon of John the Deacon, written in 875, records the merchant's astonished words when he found the bag the next morning: "It is a miracle from heaven! The gods have not abandoned us!"

The bag contained exactly the amount needed for the dowry of the eldest daughter, who shortly thereafter married an honest merchant of the city. But the story does not end there. Some time later, a second bag of gold mysteriously appeared in the same house, allowing the second daughter to marry as well.

The merchant, determined to discover the identity of his benefactor, spent the next few nights awake. When the third bag of gold passed through the window, the man rushed out into the street just in time to see a figure quickly moving away in the darkness. He recognized it immediately: it was young Nicholas.

"Why?" asked the merchant, catching up with him. "Why did you do all this in secret?"

Nicholas's answer, handed down through the centuries through the "Vita Compilata" of Michael the Archimandrite, reveals the essence of his spirituality: "Because true charity seeks neither glory nor reward. It is the joy of giving, not of receiving, that fills the heart of God."

The story quickly spread through the streets of Myra, despite Nicholas's attempts to remain anonymous. The Byzantine chronicler Symeon Metaphrastes, in the 10th century, wrote: "The rumor spread like leaves in the autumn wind, and soon there was no inhabitant of Myra who did not know the story of the three bags of gold."

But what makes this episode even more extraordinary are the details that emerge from contemporary documents. The acts of the Council of Nicaea in 325, where Nicholas was present as bishop of Myra, contain an interesting marginal note referring to this event. An Alexandrian delegate wrote: "Among us sits a man who has transformed gold into hope, not through alchemy, but through the purity of his heart."

The story of the three sisters soon became a symbol of discreet generosity and help to those most in need. In the catacombs of San Callisto in Rome, a graffito dating back to the 5th century was found depicting three overlapping circles, interpreted by scholars as a stylised representation of the three bags of gold, accompanied by the inscription in ancient Greek: "Like Nicholas in the night."

This legend has spanned the centuries, transforming and enriching itself with new meanings. In the "Legendary of Pietro Calo" of the 14th century, the three bags of gold are associated for the first time with oranges, which will then become one of the typical gifts left in Christmas stockings. The connection is not accidental: oranges, rare and precious in the medieval world, were considered "golden apples", a gift worthy of a king.

The impact of this story on popular culture was such that, over the centuries, the gesture of secret giving became a tradition throughout Europe. In Germany, until the 19th century, there was a custom of leaving small anonymous gifts in front of the doors of poor houses on the night of Saint Nicholas, December 6th.

But the true meaning of this legend goes far beyond the simple act of giving. It represents the birth of a new way of understanding Christian charity, no longer as a display of virtue, but as a silent and discreet gesture of love. The words attributed to Nicholas in a sermon from the 6th century, preserved in the monastery of Saint Catherine on Mount Sinai, perfectly summarize this concept: "The hand that gives must not make noise, because the sound of the metal would cover the voice of the heart."

The story of the three sisters therefore marks a turning point not only in Nicola's life, but in the very concept of Christian charity. It is the moment in which a simple act of generosity is transformed into a universal symbol, destined to inspire generations of believers and to lay the foundations for that figure of the nocturnal donor who, centuries later, would become Santa Claus.

A particularly touching testimony of how this story influenced people's daily lives comes from a letter found in a Cappadocian monastery, dating back to the 6th century. A young woman writes to her mother: "Every time I see three stars aligned in the night sky, I think of Nicholas's three bags of gold and remember that hope can come even in the darkest hour of the night."

THE WEEPING TOMB: THE MYSTERY OF THE HEALING FLUID

Transparent drops slide down the white marble, collecting in small crystalline pools at the base of the tomb. Pilgrims call them "manna of Saint Nicholas," an extraordinary phenomenon that has fascinated believers and scientists for centuries. But the history of this mysterious fluid begins long before the construction of the current tomb.

In 343 AD, when Nicholas breathed his last in the city of Myra, no one could have imagined that a substance with supposedly miraculous properties would flow from his tomb. The first evidence of this phenomenon dates back to a 5th-century document, preserved in the library of the monastery of St. John on Patmos. The manuscript, written by a monk named Theodosius, describes with amazement: "From the stone flows water as clear as morning dew, which heals the sick and brings relief to the suffering."

The Byzantine archaeologist Procopius of Caesarea, in his "De Aedificiis", provides a detailed description of the first tomb of Nicholas: "It was a simple sarcophagus of white marble, but the stone seemed to have a life of its own, exuding a perfumed liquid that the faithful collected in small glass vials." Some of these vials, dated between the 6th and 7th centuries, were found during archaeological excavations in the port district of Constantinople, evidence of the early diffusion of this cult.

A 7th-century Armenian pilgrim, whose diary has come down to us through a Georgian translation, wrote: "I saw with my own eyes how the marble sheds tears of healing. The air around the tomb is filled with a sweet scent, similar to that of almond blossoms in spring." The reference to the scent of almonds is not accidental: the region of Myra was famous for its orchards, and many saw in this fragrance a sign of the continuity between the saint and his land.

But the phenomenon of manna was not limited to arousing popular devotion. In the "Treatise on the Sacred Waters", compiled in the eighth century by a physician of the school of Alexandria, there is an attempt at scientific analysis: "The liquid that exudes from the tomb has peculiar properties. It does not corrupt, it maintains its clarity for months and, when applied to wounds or sores, it seems to accelerate their healing."

A particularly significant episode is recorded in the chronicles of the Myra monastery from the year 798. During a terrible epidemic that struck the city, the fluid from the tomb was distributed among the population. The chronicler notes: "Those who received the holy manna found relief from their ailments, while the disease continued to claim victims among those who had not received it."

The fame of this phenomenon attracted the attention of scholars from all over the Mediterranean world. An Arab alchemist, Al-Razi, in his "Book of Secrets", devotes an entire chapter to "the water that cries from the stone of Myra". His observations are surprisingly precise: "The liquid has a density slightly higher than ordinary water and leaves a salty residue when evaporated. It does not freeze even in the coldest months."

Over the centuries, many legends have woven themselves around this phenomenon. A 9th-century folk tale tells of a Greek merchant who attempted to steal a vial of manna to sell in Constantinople. According to legend, the liquid turned into ordinary water as soon as it left the sacred precincts of the church.

Modern analysis has revealed that the fluid does indeed contain a variety of dissolved minerals, some of which have natural antiseptic properties. But that hasn't diminished the mystery surrounding the phenomenon. As Byzantine historian John Freely writes: "Science can explain the composition of the fluid, but not why it continues to flow after more than fifteen hundred years."

An 11th-century illuminated manuscript in the Vatican Library shows a miniature of the tomb surrounded by pilgrims collecting the precious liquid in small silver vials. The caption reads, "Hic fons vitae ex petra fluit" (Here the fountain of life flows from the stone), a reference that links the phenomenon to the biblical tradition of water flowing from the rock in the desert.

In 1087, when sailors from Bari transferred the relics of Saint Nicholas to their city, their main concern was whether the miracle of the manna would continue in the new burial. A contemporary chronicler reports the words of one of the sailors: "If the saint wants to follow us, the stone will continue to cry even in Bari."

Particularly touching is the testimony of a Sicilian woman, contained in a letter from the 12th century: "I took my son, blind from birth, to the tomb of the saint. I bathed his eyes with the holy manna and, while I prayed, I saw his eyelids tremble. When he opened them, for the first time he could see my face."

The phenomenon of manna helped create a special bond between the saint and the element of water. It is no coincidence that Saint Nicholas became the protector of sailors: the miraculous water flowing from his tomb seemed to be a tangible sign of his ability to master this element.

Medieval chronicles report numerous cases of miraculous healings attributed to manna. A 13th-century register, preserved in the archives of the cathedral of Bari, methodically lists the miracles verified: "Anno Domini 1256: a paralyzed child began to walk again. Anno Domini 1257: a mute woman regained her speech. Anno Domini 1258: a fisherman bitten by a poisonous snake was healed in three days."

But perhaps the real miracle lies not so much in the alleged healings, but in the continuity of a phenomenon that, century after century, continues to inspire wonder and hope. As an anonymous poet of the 14th century wrote: "It is not the water that heals, but the faith that it represents. It is not the stone that cries, but the heart that opens to wonder."

The mystery of the weeping tomb remains one of the most fascinating aspects of the story of Saint Nicholas, a phenomenon that defies rational explanations and continues to intertwine science and faith, history and legend, in a tale that is renewed every day, drop after drop, like the fluid that continues to flow from the sacred stone.

CHAPTER 2: THE HOLY TRAVELER

FROM MYRA TO BARI: THE THEFT OF THE SACRED RELICS

On the night of May 9-10, 1087, sixty-two sailors from Bari moved stealthily through the shadows of Myra's harbor. Their goal was not gold or precious spices, but something far more sacred: the relics of Saint Nicholas. The city, once a thriving Christian center, now lay in a state of semi-abandonedness under the rule of the Seljuk Turks. The ancient walls, silent witnesses to centuries of history, seemed to whisper warnings to the sailors who approached the basilica with hearts in their throats.

"May God forgive us," murmured Matthew, the youngest of the group, as they forced their way into the church. The chronicon of the time, written by the monk Nicephorus, tells how the sailors had to overcome the resistance of four monks who guarded the holy sepulchre. "Do not desecrate this holy place!" one of the monks shouted in Greek, but his words fell on deaf ears. The people of Bari were determined: the saint's relics had to be saved from the Muslim danger and taken to a safe place.

The air was thick with incense as the sailors finally reached the tomb. The marble floor, worn by centuries of kneeling pilgrims, dimly reflected the light of their torches. With crude tools they began to dig around the sarcophagus. The sound of metal against stone echoed ominously in the empty basilica as the sailors worked feverishly, knowing that dawn might bring the discovery of their sacred theft.

"A miracle!" exclaimed one of the sailors when, having broken the seal of the tomb, a very sweet scent spread through the air. It was the holy manna, the miraculous liquid that according to tradition still oozes from the bones of the saint. The chronicles of the time report how this perfumed liquid was considered tangible proof of Nicholas' sanctity, capable of healing illnesses and performing miracles.

The testimony of John the Archdeacon, present that night, describes in great detail the opening of the sarcophagus: "The sacred bones lay immersed in a crystalline liquid, like precious pearls in a sea of purity". The sailors, with trembling hands, collected the relics, wrapping them in precious silk drapes. Not all of the body was removed: some minor bones remained in the tomb, perhaps because of haste, perhaps because of a tacit compromise with the monks who were crying for the loss of their most precious treasure.

The return journey to Bari was full of tension. The relics were hidden in the ship's hold, protected by bales of straw and cotton. The sailors, expert connoisseurs of the sea, continually scanned the horizon fearing the pursuit of Byzantine ships or, worse still, the attack of Saracen pirates who infested those waters. The sea was rough, but according to the chronicles of the time, every time the waves threatened to overwhelm the vessel, it was enough to invoke Saint Nicholas to see the waters miraculously calm down.

The arrival in Bari, on May 9, 1087, was triumphant. The entire city poured into the port to welcome the sacred relics. The bells rang out in celebration and Archbishop Ursone, accompanied by the clergy and the city authorities, welcomed the precious cargo with full honors. The chronicler Orderico Vitale recounts how "the joy of the people was mixed with tears, while an interminable procession accompanied the relics through the streets of the city".

The bones were temporarily deposited in the church of Saint Eustachius, while it was decided where to build a basilica worthy of housing them. It was Abbot Elia, the future archbishop of Bari, who supervised the construction of the new church. The work proceeded at a rapid pace, supported by generous donations from the faithful and merchants of Bari. The crypt was completed in just two years, a record time for the time, allowing the final translation of the relics on October 1, 1089.

The impact of this "sacred theft" was enormous. Bari immediately became one of the main pilgrimage centers of Christianity, second only to Rome and Santiago de Compostela. Devotion to Saint Nicholas, already strong in the East, spread rapidly throughout the West. Pilgrims flocked from all over Europe, attracted by the fame of the miracles performed by the saint and by the holy manna that continued to flow from his bones.

The transfer of the relics also marked an important moment of contact between East and West. The Basilica of Saint Nicholas in Bari became a meeting point between the two souls of Christianity, so much so that even today it is one of the few places in the West where Orthodox Christians can celebrate their rites. The architecture of the church itself reflects this fusion, combining typically Western Romanesque elements with Byzantine influences.

But not everyone celebrated this "pious theft". In Constantinople, Emperor Alexius I Comnenus expressed his indignation at what he considered a sacrilegious theft. The monks of Myra, deprived of their most precious treasure, continued to demand the return of the relics for a long time. Even today, in the basilica of Myra, one can see the empty sarcophagus of Saint Nicholas, a silent testimony to that night in May 1087.

The translation of the relics of Saint Nicholas was much more than a simple transfer of sacred relics. It was an event that profoundly marked the history of Christian devotion and helped spread the cult of the saint throughout the West. As one historian of the time wrote, "The bones of Nicholas left the East to conquer the West, just as his spirit would later conquer the entire world."

The consequences of that May night still reverberate today. The Basilica of Saint Nicholas in Bari continues to be a place of pilgrimage for believers of every Christian denomination. Orthodox and Catholics kneel before the same tomb, a living testimony to how the figure of Saint Nicholas has transcended the boundaries of religious divisions. And every December 6, when the saint's feast day is celebrated, the city of Bari relives that ancient story, while the scent of holy manna continues to spread from the crypt, just like that night almost a thousand years ago.

THE SPREAD OF THE CULT IN EUROPE

Through the mists of the Middle Ages, the cult of Saint Nicholas spread throughout Europe like a river that, starting from Bari, branched out into a thousand streams, touching cities and villages, castles and monasteries. The arrival of his relics in the Apulian city was only the beginning of an extraordinary spiritual adventure that would transform the saint of Myra into one of the most venerated figures of medieval Christianity.

In 1095, shortly after the relics arrived in the capital of Puglia, Pope Urban II called for the First Crusade from the very crypt where the bones of the saint rested. It was no coincidence: the crusaders adopted Saint Nicholas as their protector, bringing his cult to the most remote places in Europe. A Norman knight, in a diary found centuries later, wrote: "Wherever we go, the name of Nicholas precedes us like a banner of hope."

The Mediterranean trade routes became the main channels for this diffusion. Venetian merchants, historical rivals of the Bari people, did not want to be outdone. In 1100, they managed to steal some relics that had remained in Myra, bringing them to their city. A chronicler of the time, Marco da Venezia, recounts: "The bones of the saint gave off such a sweet scent that the sailors forgot the stench of the bilge for days".

In the Germanic lands, the cult of St. Nicholas found fertile ground thanks to Princess Theophanu, wife of Emperor Otto II. The Byzantine noblewoman brought with her not only precious relics of the saint, but also the traditions and legends surrounding him. In the monastery of Reichenau, a monk noted in 1120: "Devotion to the Eastern saint grows like ivy on our walls, enveloping every aspect of everyday life."

Medieval universities played a major role in spreading the cult. In Paris, Oxford, and Bologna, St. Nicholas became the patron saint of students. A tradition born in Paris in 1175 saw poor students go from door to door on December 6, singing hymns to the saint and receiving food and coins in return. "We sing for Nicholas, friend of poor scholars," went an ancient student chant transcribed in a manuscript from the Sorbonne.

Medieval art was enriched with representations of the saint. The frescoes in the lower basilica of Assisi, made around 1310, show Saint Nicholas in the act of giving the three bags of gold to the poor girls. Giotto painted the scene with such realism that, according to a Franciscan chronicle, "the pilgrims stretched out their hands toward the fresco, believing they could touch the gold coins".

In the coastal regions of Northern Europe, sailors adopted Saint Nicholas as their protector. In the port of Hamburg, a merchants' guild built a church dedicated to the saint in 1195. The guild book contains a touching prayer: "As you saved the sailors in the storm, O Nicholas, protect our ships and bring our men home safe and sound."

Medieval Russia embraced the cult of St. Nicholas with particular fervor. In 1165, Prince Mstislav built a church in Novgorod dedicated to the saint, which became one of the major pilgrimage centers in the Slavic world. A 13th-century pilgrim wrote: "In Novgorod, Nicholas is not only a saint, he is like a father to all Russians, rich and poor."

Legends about the saint multiplied and were enriched with local details. In Lorraine, it was said that Saint Nicholas had resurrected three children killed by an evil butcher. This story, absent in the first hagiographies, became so popular that the saint was often depicted with three children in a tub. A 14th-century storyteller, quoted in a Nancy manuscript, sang: "Thrice blessed be Nicholas, who gives back children to weeping mothers."

In the Celtic world, the cult of Saint Nicholas was intertwined with ancient local traditions. In Ireland, the monks of Clonmacnoise wrote down a story in 1250 that fused the miracle of the three bags of gold with the legends of leprechauns: "Like the little green men, Nicholas brings gold to those in need, but he does so in the light of day, not in the shadows."

Popular devotion took on increasingly elaborate forms. In Salisbury, England, a festival was celebrated in 1300 in which a child was elected "Bishop of St. Nicholas" and symbolically governed the diocese for a day. The cathedral register records that "the little bishop blesses the crowd with the same grace as the saint he imitates."

In Italy, each region developed its own traditions related to the saint. In Verona, in 1280, a group of nuns began the tradition of distributing sweets to poor children on the day of Saint Nicholas. Their recipe book, which miraculously survived, contains the recipe for the "saint's biscuits": "They must be sweet like his charity and golden like his heart."

Medieval guilds sought the protection of St. Nicholas. Pharmacists chose him as their patron because, according to a 13th-century legend, he healed a child with three drops of blessed oil. In Siena, the register of the pharmacists' guild from 1340 records a prayer: "As Nicholas' oil heals the body, may his blessing heal our souls."

With the advent of the Gothic, cathedrals dedicated to Saint Nicholas became increasingly imposing. The cathedral of Fribourg, begun in 1283, features a cycle of stained glass windows that narrate the life of the saint. A master glassmaker noted in his notebook: "The colors must be as brilliant as his faith, and the light that filters must recall the brightness of his miracles."

By the end of the Middle Ages, the cult of Saint Nicholas was so deeply rooted in Europe that there was hardly a city without a church or chapel dedicated to him. As a Flemish chronicler wrote in 1450: "From the North Sea to the Mediterranean, from the lands of the

Slavs to the borders of Ireland, the name of Nicholas resounds like a song of hope and charity."

This process of diffusion laid the foundations for the saint's subsequent transformations. In every region, in every city, Saint Nicholas took on local characteristics while maintaining intact his fundamental message of generosity and protection of the weak. Like a seed carried by the wind, his cult had taken root in different soils, giving rise to unique traditions that, in the following centuries, would contribute to the birth of new and surprising incarnations of his figure.

THE MANY FACES OF SAINT NICHOLAS: PROTECTOR OF CHILDREN, SAILORS AND MERCHANTS

Along the crowded docks of the port of Venice in 1323, a merchant recorded a strange story in his diary. During a storm in the Aegean Sea, when all hope seemed lost, the crew had invoked Saint Nicholas. "As if by miracle," the merchant wrote, "a luminous figure appeared on the bow, and the waves instantly calmed. No one on board doubted that it was the saint of Myra who had come to our rescue."

Few figures in the history of Christianity have been able to embody such diverse roles as Saint Nicholas. In a manuscript preserved in the Abbey of Montecassino, dated 1256, a Benedictine monk lists more than thirty categories of people who considered the saint as their protector: "It is as if Nicholas had the gift of ubiquity, being everywhere where his help is needed".

The protection of children remains perhaps the most famous and touching aspect of his patronage. In 1340, in Cologne, a desperate mother left a votive offering in the church of St. Nicholas: a small silver shoe with an inscription that read "For my son Thomas, whom you saved from the malignant fever." The tradition of leaving shoes for St. Nicholas arose from these gestures of gratitude.

In the ports of the Mediterranean, every ship that set sail carried an image of the saint in the cockpit. A Genoese captain of the 15th century had a Saint Nicholas calming the storms painted on his ship, accompanied by the inscription: "Navigamus sub tuo praesidio" (We sail under your protection). The maritime archives of Genoa preserve hundreds of testimonies of miracles attributed to the saint at sea.

In the world of commerce, Saint Nicholas was venerated as a guarantor of honesty and prosperity. In Bruges, in 1378, the merchants' guild built a chapel dedicated to the saint, where each new member had to swear to conduct his business honestly, invoking Saint Nicholas as a witness. The guild book contains a prayer that read: "As you have multiplied the grain to feed the poor, O Nicholas, multiply our honest trade."

The protection of students was another fundamental aspect of his cult. At the University of Paris, in 1280, the "Saint Nicholas Scholarship" was established, a fund to help poor students. A document of the time reports the words of a young student: "Thanks to the saint who was bishop of Myra, I was able to continue my studies. As he gave three gold scholarships to poor girls, so he gave me the opportunity to study".

Young women looking for a husband invoked him with particular devotion. In Verona, in 1412, a curious tradition was born:

marriageable girls went to the church of San Nicola and threw a gold coin into the baptismal font. If the coin jingled in a certain way, it was said that the marriage would take place within the year. A chronicle of the time reports: "Coins that fall silently bring tears, those that sing bring weddings".

Medieval pharmacists considered him their patron because of the miraculous oil that oozed from his relics. In Salerno, at the first medical school in Europe, a 1290 treatise describes the healing properties of the "manna of Saint Nicholas": "This holy oil heals the body as his intercession heals the soul." Pharmacists prepared ointments by mixing medicinal herbs with a few drops of the oil from Bari.

Even thieves, paradoxically, considered him their protector, not to promote theft, but to repent and find redemption. A 14th-century story tells of a thief from Padua who, after praying to St. Nicholas, returned everything he had stolen and became an honest craftsman. In his will, preserved in the city archives, he wrote: "I owe my salvation to Nicholas, who showed me the path of honesty."

Bakers venerated him for the miracle of the multiplied grain. In Strasbourg, in 1360, the bakers' guild commissioned a statue of the saint representing him with three loaves in his hand. Tradition required that each baker, before starting work at dawn, recite a prayer in front of the statue: "As you fed Myra in famine, bless our daily work."

The prisoners invoked him as a liberator. In the archives of the Republic of Venice there is a testimony of a merchant, dated 1398, who tells of his miraculous liberation from Turkish prisons: "I saw Saint Nicholas in a dream, and when I awoke the chains were broken". In medieval prisons it was not uncommon to find small altars dedicated to the saint.

The lawyers' guilds chose him as their protector for his sense of justice. In Bologna, in 1400, the college of lawyers had a fresco painted representing Saint Nicholas in the act of saving three innocent people from the death sentence. The inscription read: "Patron of those who seek justice, defender of the innocent".

But perhaps the most surprising aspect of his patronage concerned perfumers. In Grasse, Provence, the center of medieval perfumery, a 15th-century perfumers' guild had chosen Saint Nicholas as their patron because of the miraculous scent emanating from his relics. A 1445 recipe book describes a perfume called "Essence of Saint Nicholas," created to replicate the scent of holy manna.

The versatility of his patronage was also reflected in his art. A Florentine painter of the 1430s created a polyptych in which each panel depicted a different aspect of the saint's protection: "As a diamond has many faces," he wrote in his description of the work, "so Nicholas reflects the divine light in a thousand different ways."

This multiplicity of roles and protections has helped make Saint Nicholas a universal figure, able to speak to people of every social condition and profession. As a Venetian chronicler wrote in 1450: "There is no category of people who cannot find in Nicholas a protector, there is no need to which he cannot respond, there is no prayer to which he does not listen with benevolence."

St. Nicholas's ability to be all things to all people, while still maintaining his identity as a charitable and just bishop, paved the way for his later transformation into an even more universal figure. But that is a story for later chapters of our narrative.

THE TRANSFORMATION FROM SAINT TO MAGICAL FIGURE

In the darkness of a medieval church, amid the smoke of candles and the smell of incense, a believer kneels before the icon of St. Nicholas. His lips murmur a prayer, while outside, in the winter night, the Saint is said to ride across the rooftops, bringing gifts to children. This dual nature of St. Nicholas - a venerated saint of the Church and a magical figure of popular folklore - represents one of the most fascinating paradoxes in European religious history.

The transformation of Saint Nicholas from a historical figure to a supernatural being did not occur at a specific moment, but was the result of centuries of cultural and spiritual evolution. A 12th-century manuscript, found in the Abbey of Saint-Denis near Paris, contains a curious annotation: "People whisper that on the night of Saint Nicholas, the saint himself visits the homes of the faithful, leaving small gifts for virtuous children." This testimony represents one of the first written records of the gradual metamorphosis of the saint into a figure with supernatural powers.

During the 13th century, while the relics of Saint Nicholas in Bari attracted pilgrims from all over Europe, increasingly fantastic stories about him spread in the northern regions. A German chronicler of the time, Heinrich von Kleist, noted with disappointment how "peasants tell their children that Saint Nicholas can walk through walls and appear in several places at once." The Church initially tried to counter these popular beliefs, considering them dangerously close to pagan superstition.

Legends of the saint began to incorporate increasingly elaborate supernatural elements. A 14th-century folk tale from the Friesland region tells of how St. Nicholas had the power to ride across the sky on a white horse, accompanied by ravens who whispered the names of good and bad children in his ear. This story has striking parallels with ancient Germanic legends of Odin, highlighting how pagan traditions gradually merged with Christian worship of the saint.

A crucial moment in this transformation occurred during the great famine of 1315-1317. In those years of despair, stories multiplied of mysterious nocturnal apparitions of the saint, who left bread and provisions in the homes of the poorest. A document from the time, preserved in the archives of Bruges, reports the testimony of a widow: "I was without food for my children, when on the night of Saint Nicholas I found a basket full of bread on the doorstep. No trace in the snow, as if it had come down from heaven".

The merchant guilds contributed significantly to this development. Merchants, who considered Saint Nicholas their patron saint, began to organize elaborate celebrations in his honor, during which a person dressed as the saint distributed gifts to poor children. A Hamburg trade register from 1348 describes one such celebration: "For the feast of Saint Nicholas, the merchant Johannes Müller dressed up as the saint, with a white beard and red cloak, and distributed apples and nuts to the children of the port."

The Protestant Reformation, paradoxically, instead of eliminating these practices, contributed to strengthening the magical aspects of the figure of Saint Nicholas. In the regions that embraced Protestantism, the saint was gradually stripped of his religious attributes, but he maintained and even strengthened his supernatural characteristics. A Lutheran pastor from Hamburg, in 1580, complained that "despite the purification of the true faith, the people continue to believe that Saint Nicholas flies at night to leave gifts to children".

Popular beliefs began to attribute increasingly extraordinary powers to the saint. In some regions of the Netherlands, it was believed that he could transform himself into a ray of light to enter homes through closed windows. In other areas, it was said that he possessed a magic book in which all the children's behaviors during the year were written. A Flemish manuscript from the 16th century says: "The saint knows every thought of children, sees through walls and can be in a hundred places at once."

The most significant transformation occurred in the way people imagined the saint's physical appearance. From the severe Byzantine icons, the image of St. Nicholas gradually evolved into that of a more human and approachable figure. A fresco from 1485 in the St. Nicholas Church in Wismar already shows him with a long white beard and a cloak decorated with stars, much more similar to later representations of Sinterklaas than to the austere Bishop of Myra.

Of particular interest is a document from 1602, from a small town in the Rhineland, which describes a procession in honor of Saint Nicholas: "The saint appeared on a chariot drawn by white horses, his cloak was covered with artificial snowflakes and he carried a large sack full of gifts. The children firmly believed that he had flown in from heaven." This description shows how, by the beginning of the 17th century, many elements of the future figure of Santa Claus were already present in popular imagination.

Stories about the saint began to include increasingly fanciful details about his abode. A Dutch folk tale from 1620 claimed that St. Nicholas lived in an ice palace "beyond the northern lands, where the snow never melts." This location surprisingly foreshadows Santa Claus's future placement at the North Pole.

Finally, a crucial element of this transformation was the gradual shift in emphasis from the traditional miracles attributed to the saint to his function as a gift-giver. A prayer book from 1650 from the Cologne library contains this significant annotation: "Children no longer pray to Saint Nicholas for his intercession with God, but to receive his magical gifts." This shift reflected a broader social and cultural transformation, where the material aspects of giving began to prevail over the spiritual ones.

In this complex evolution, Saint Nicholas never completely lost his religious dimension, but acquired a new identity as a magical figure of popular folklore. This transformation prepared the ground for the subsequent evolution towards Sinterklaas and, finally, Santa Claus, demonstrating how religious and popular traditions can merge and transform over the centuries, creating new meanings and new forms of celebration.

CHAPTER 3: THE JOURNEY NORTH

ARRIVING IN THE NETHERLANDS: THE BIRTH OF SINTERKLAAS

In the mists of an autumn morning in 1150, a merchant ship sailed across the North Sea toward Amsterdam. On board, among the precious goods from the Mediterranean, there was also something intangible: the stories of Saint Nicholas, destined to be profoundly transformed in the new territory that awaited them.

Dutch merchants trading with southern Italy could not have imagined that, along with their merchandise, they were importing to the Netherlands a tradition that would change the face of Christmas forever. An ancient customs register from the port of Amsterdam, dated 1156, lists among the incoming goods "a wooden statue of Saint Nicholas, commissioned by the Merchants' Guild". This could be one of the first documents attesting to the physical arrival of the cult of the saint in the Dutch lands.

The port cities of the Netherlands proved to be particularly fertile ground for the cult of Saint Nicholas. A contemporary chronicler, Willem van Utrecht, wrote in his diary of 1175: "The sailors swear that during storms they see the luminous figure of the saint walking on the water, guiding the ships to safe harbor." This testimony reveals how already in the early years the figure of the saint was taking on distinctive local characteristics.

The linguistic transformation from "Saint Nicholas" to "Sinterklaas" represents more than a simple change in pronunciation. A document from around 1200, preserved in the library of Utrecht, uses the term "Sinter Niklaas" for the first time, revealing how the saint's name was already undergoing the phonetic metamorphosis that would make him unique in the Dutch cultural landscape.

Of particular interest is a story in the Dordrecht city chronicle from 1235, which tells how a rich merchant, inspired by the stories of the saint, began to distribute gold coins to poor children during the night of December 5, leaving them in their shoes. "And since no one saw him do this," the chronicle says, "the people began to believe that it was Sinterklaas himself who was bringing the gifts."

During the 13th century, Dutch cities began to organize elaborate celebrations in honor of Sinterklaas. A municipal document from Delft from 1287 describes a procession in which "a man dressed as the saint, with mitre and crozier, rode through the city on a white steed, blessing the crowd and distributing spices and sweets to the children." This description represents one of the first documented examples of the physical personification of Sinterklaas.

The merchant guilds played a key role in establishing this tradition. A register of the Amsterdam Merchants' Guild from 1300 states that "on the feast of Sinterklaas, every merchant shall contribute two guilders to the purchase of gifts for the children of the orphanage." This institutionalized practice helped to deeply root the figure of Sinterklaas in Dutch society.

A particular aspect of the transformation of Saint Nicholas into Sinterklaas was the emergence of a precise chronology of celebrations. A 1350 almanac from the city of Haarlem specifies that "the celebrations begin on the evening of December 5th and continue until dawn the following day, when the children find the gifts in their shoes." This tradition has remained unchanged to the present day.

The earliest artistic representations of Sinterklaas in the Netherlands already show a significant divergence from the traditional iconography of Saint Nicholas. A fresco from 1375 in the church of Saint Nicholas in Amsterdam depicts him with a red cloak embroidered with gold and a long white beard, "more like a Nordic sage than a Mediterranean bishop," as one contemporary art historian notes.

The connection between Sinterklaas and navigation has always remained very strong. A logbook from 1420 tells how Dutch sailors were convinced that the saint arrived every year from Spain on a ship loaded with gifts. This belief crystallized in popular tradition, so much so that even today it is said that Sinterklaas arrives by sea from Spain.

The figure of Sinterklaas gradually acquired unique characteristics that distinguished him from the original Saint Nicholas. A manuscript from 1460 describes how "the saint rides over the roofs of the houses on the night of December 5, listening through the chimneys to know if the children have been good." This image of a supernatural being who observes and judges the behavior of children became a central element of the tradition.

Wealthy families in the 15th century began to organize elaborate household celebrations. A family diary from 1485 describes how "on Sinterklaas evening, after the children have gone to bed, the servants place the shoes in front of the fireplace, filling them with nuts, apples and sweets. In the morning, the children find the gifts and are convinced that the saint has passed by during the night."

A distinctive element of Dutch tradition was the use of special sweets associated with Sinterklaas. A recipe book from 1500 contains the first mention of "speculaas", spiced biscuits in the shape of the saint that are still an integral part of the celebrations today. The recipe specifies that "the biscuits should be shaped with the image of Sinterklaas, so that children can recognize the saint's gifts".

The educational and moral aspect of the figure of Sinterklaas emerges clearly in a parenting manual from 1550, which recommends "using the figure of the saint as an example of virtue and generosity, reminding children that Sinterklaas only rewards those who behave well". This pedagogical aspect of the tradition would be maintained in the following centuries.

Towards the end of the 16th century, with the arrival of the Protestant Reformation in the Netherlands, the figure of Sinterklaas was in danger of disappearing. However, as one contemporary observer noted in 1580, "despite the Protestant preachers condemning the cult of saints, the people do not want to give up Sinterklaas, seeing in him not so much a saint of the Church as a magical benefactor of children."

The survival and transformation of Sinterklaas in the Netherlands is a fascinating example of how a religious tradition can evolve and adapt, retaining some of its original elements while acquiring new ones. This figure, born from the fusion of the Bishop of Myra and Nordic traditions, would in turn have profoundly influenced the development of the figure of Santa Claus, demonstrating how cultural traditions are constantly evolving.

DUTCH TRADITIONS: BLACK PETER AND THE SHOES ON THE FIREPLACE

In the dark of a December night in 1350, in a small house in Amsterdam, a mother whispered to her children: "Remember to polish your clogs well before you put them in front of the fireplace, because Zwarte Piet has watchful eyes and reports everything to Sinterklaas." This simple domestic scene contains two of the most characteristic elements of Dutch tradition: the enigmatic figure of Zwarte Piet (Black Peter) and the ritual of the shoes in the fireplace.

An old municipal register from Utrecht from 1351 contains the first documented mention of this mysterious figure: "On the feast of St. Nicholas, a man with a face blackened by soot accompanies the saint, carrying a sack for gifts and a register of the children's behavior." This first description of what would become Zwarte Piet already contained the essential elements of the character.

The practice of leaving shoes in front of the fireplace has its roots in an even older custom. A manuscript from the monastery of Egmond, dated 1280, describes how "the poor would leave their clogs outside the church door, hoping that some kind soul would deposit food or coins in them." Over time, this tradition merged with the cult of Sinterklaas, moving from the churchyard to the hearth.

During the 14th century, celebrations became increasingly elaborate. A 1375 document from the Delft merchants' guild describes a procession in which "a Moor dressed in colored silk precedes the saint, throwing sweet pepernoten to the children and jokingly threatening to carry off the naughty ones in his sack." This is one of the first detailed descriptions of Zwarte Piet's role in public celebrations.

The shoes at the fireplace took on a special meaning in Dutch tradition. A family memoir from 1420 recounts: "On the evening of December 5, the children fill their hooves with hay and carrots for Sinterklaas's horse. In the morning, they find the hay eaten and in its place sweets and toys." This symbolic exchange strengthened the bond between the children and the magical figure of the saint.

The figure of Zwarte Piet gradually became richer in details and distinctive features. A diary from 1460 describes how "the black servant of the saint wears sumptuous clothes in the Spanish manner, with feathers in his hat and gold earrings". This description reflects the influence of Spanish rule in the Netherlands and the increasing elaboration of the character.

An interesting aspect emerges from an Amsterdam tax document of 1495, which records the purchase of "exotic spices and oriental sweets for the sacks of Zwarte Piet". This detail reveals how the character was associated with the spice trade and maritime connections with distant lands, central elements of the Dutch economy of the time.

The household traditions associated with these celebrations are detailed in a 1520 household handbook: "On Christmas Eve, parents should have their children sing traditional Sinterklaas songs while they arrange their clogs. Then, when everyone is asleep, they fill the shoes with surprises, making sure to leave soot prints around the fireplace as proof that Zwarte Piet has passed by."

A particular element of the tradition emerges from a letter from 1555, in which a mother writes to her sister: "The children believe that Zwarte Piet can climb on roofs and down chimneys to spy on their behavior during the year. This belief makes them behave better, although I confess that I use this threat more often than I should."

The practice of writing letters to Sinterklaas, by inserting them into the clogs, is first documented in a diary from 1580: "My daughter wrote her hopes and wishes on a sheet of paper, which she carefully folded and placed in her clog along with a carrot for the saint's horse." This custom demonstrates how the tradition continued to evolve, incorporating new elements.

During the 17th century, celebrations became increasingly elaborate. An account from 1625 describes how "wealthy families would organize veritable treasure hunts, with Zwarte Piet leaving rhyming clues hidden in various places around the house, ultimately leading the children to their gifts." This practice shows the evolution of the tradition into increasingly sophisticated forms of entertainment.

Pepernoten, small spiced biscuits, became an essential part of the celebration. A recipe from 1650 specifies that "real pepernoten must contain black pepper, cinnamon and nutmeg, spices that Zwarte Piet brings directly from the East Indies." This connection with exotic spices reinforced the aura of mystery and magic around the character.

Fueling the tradition is a school register from 1675: "The teacher has ordered that each child leave a clog under the teacher's desk during Sinterklaas week. Every morning, the most deserving find a small gift, while the negligent receive a twig, a sign that Zwarte Piet has reported their laziness to the saint."

The tradition has remained surprisingly intact through the centuries, as a comparison of 18th-century descriptions with earlier ones shows. A diary from 1720 describes a scene almost identical to that of 1350: "The children carefully polished their hooves, sang traditional songs and left carrots and hay for the horse. The next morning, the excitement of finding the gifts was indescribable."

Public celebrations took on increasingly grandiose proportions. A newspaper article from 1785 describes the arrival of Sinterklaas in Amsterdam: "A decorated ship arrived in the harbor, with the saint and his entourage of Zwarte Pieten. The crowd of children was so large that the guards had difficulty maintaining order as the Pieten threw sweets and small gifts."

Over time, these traditions have become so deeply rooted in Dutch culture that they have become an integral part of the national identity. As one English observer wrote in 1815: "The Dutch can give up many things, but never the magic of Sinterklaas and the rituals that go with him. The shoes by the fireplace and the figure of Zwarte Piet are more than mere traditions: they are the very heart of their Christmas celebration."

THE CONNECTION WITH ODIN: WHITE HORSES AND NIGHT HUNTS

In the cold winters of Northern Europe, when the icy winds sweep the snowy plains and the sun quickly disappears behind the horizon, the ancient tales come to life. Legends are intertwined like the branches of ancient trees, and in this intertwining we can find one of the most fascinating connections in the story of the transformation of Saint Nicholas: his connection with Odin, the father of the gods in Norse mythology.

In the village of Kirkjubø, on the Faroe Islands, an ancient 12th-century manuscript tells of how locals saw a mysterious figure riding across the sky during the darkest winter nights. "It was as if the sky itself opened," writes the anonymous chronicler, "and through that cleft rode a rider on a steed as white as the purest snow." This description, strikingly similar to that of Odin on his eight-legged horse, Sleipnir, overlaps almost perfectly with the legends that circulated at the same time about Saint Nicholas.

The fusion of these two figures was not accidental. In the process of Christianizing the Nordic lands, missionaries faced a dilemma: how to make the new Christian saints accepted by populations deeply attached to their gods? The solution was as ingenious as it was natural: to allow a gradual overlap between the sacred figures, maintaining some elements of the ancient traditions while introducing new ones.

Odin, in Norse tradition, led the Wild Hunt, a ghostly procession that traversed the heavens during Yuletide, the ancient Germanic holiday that coincided with the winter solstice. During these nocturnal journeys, the god was believed to leave gifts or punishments for mortals. Villagers would leave hay and carrots for Sleipnir in their shoes by the hearth—a tradition that has surprising echoes in modern Christmas customs.

"In the dead of winter, when Odin rides," says an ancient 10th-century Icelandic poem, "wise children fill their boots with sweet straw for his steed. In return, the Allfather leaves them gifts of honey and nuts." This practice survived Christianization, becoming the tradition of leaving shoes by the fireplace for Saint Nicholas.

The process of merging the two figures was facilitated by some striking similarities. Both were wise father figures, both traveled through the heavens, both brought gifts. Odin was often depicted with a long white beard and a dark blue cloak, attributes that would later be associated with Saint Nicholas in Northern European representations.

A particularly interesting document, preserved in the library of the Abbey of St. Gallen in Switzerland, dated 1108, describes how a missionary monk in the northern lands observed that "the locals accept the saint more easily when he reminds them of the Wanderer," referring to one of the names by which Odin was known. The monk goes on to describe how he had deliberately emphasized certain aspects of the story of St. Nicholas that resonated with local beliefs.

The tradition of the white horse is particularly significant. In rural areas of northern Germany and Denmark, it was common until the 19th century to believe that Saint Nicholas rode in on a white steed. Children would leave bundles of hay not only in their shoes, but also outside the stable doors. A Danish almanac from 1784 reports: "On the night of Saint Nicholas, the little ones prepare hay for his horse, hoping that the saint will remember them with sweets and nuts."

This fusion of traditions is also reflected in clothing. Odin's blue cloak gradually evolved into the winter cloak of St. Nicholas, which in Norse depictions often included elements of Odin's ceremonial robes. A 13th-century fresco in Højby Church, Denmark, shows St. Nicholas wearing a cloak decorated with Christianized runes, a clear example of religious syncretism.

The similarities extended to the characters of the two figures. Just as Odin was known to test mortals by appearing as a traveler to test their hospitality, so St. Nicholas was famous for his tests of generosity. A 12th-century Norwegian folktale tells of how the saint, disguised as a beggar, visited homes at night to test the goodness of children.

But perhaps the most fascinating aspect of this cultural fusion is the way it influenced the concept of sacred time. The time of Yule, which was the time of Odin's Wild Hunt, overlapped perfectly with the Christian Advent period, when the feast of St. Nicholas was celebrated. This temporal overlap allowed the traditions to blend naturally, creating a rich fabric of beliefs that still influences our Christmas celebrations today.

An ancient Orkney folk song, written down in 1443 by a local monk, captures this fusion perfectly: "The holy stranger rides through the night, as once did the god of the fathers, but now he brings peace instead of war, and gifts instead of doom." These verses testify to how the local people were aware of the transformation taking place, while accepting it as a natural evolution of their traditions.

The influence of this cultural union extended well beyond the medieval period. In rural Scandinavia, until the early 20th century, it was common to refer to St. Nicholas as "the Winter Wanderer," a clear reference to Odin. Families continued to leave offerings of food and drink, no longer to appease a warrior god, but to thank a generous saint.

Through this process of religious and cultural syncretism, elements of ancient pagan traditions have survived, transforming and adapting to new contexts. Odin's white horse can still be glimpsed in Santa's flying reindeer, just as the ancient practice of leaving offerings survives in the modern custom of preparing cookies and milk for Santa Claus.

The Fusion of Christianity and Pagan Traditions

In the ancient abbey of Reichenau on the shores of Lake Constance, an 11th-century monk meticulously noted a phenomenon he was observing: "It is remarkable how our converts keep alive their ancient customs, now dyeing them with the colors of our faith." This seemingly simple observation captures the essence of one of the most fascinating processes in the history of Christianity: the gradual fusion of pagan traditions with the new Christian faith.

During the Dark Ages of the Middle Ages, as Northern Europe slowly converted to Christianity, an incredible cultural alchemy was taking place. In a manuscript preserved at the Abbey of St. Gall, dated 967, we find the testimony of a frustrated missionary: "The new Christians continue to celebrate their pagan festivals, but now they invoke the name of St. Nicholas instead of their old gods." This note reveals the complexity of the conversion process and the clever strategy adopted by the Church.

In the village of Hedeby, in present-day Denmark, archaeologists have unearthed a peculiar artifact: a 10th-century runestone that features a hybrid carving, where the figure of St. Nicholas visually overlaps with that of Thor. This find is a tangible testimony to how local people were trying to reconcile their old beliefs with the new faith.

The festival of Yule, celebrated at the time of the winter solstice, offers one of the most obvious examples of this fusion. An Anglo-Saxon chronicler of 1023 writes: "The peasants still light Yule fires, but now they say they do it to warm the infant Jesus." The Church, with pragmatic wisdom, instead of prohibiting these practices, reinterpreted them in a Christian way. The Yule tree, decorated with garlands to honor the spirits of nature, gradually became the Christmas tree, and the offerings to the gods were transformed into Christmas gifts.

A particularly revealing document comes from a 9th-century Irish monastery: "The Druids celebrated the return of light at the solstice. We now celebrate the birth of the True Light on those same days. The people understand the truth best when it speaks the language of their fathers." This reflection illuminates the Church's conscious strategy of incorporating pagan elements to facilitate conversion.

In northern Germany, an ancient tradition involved children leaving food offerings for Wodan during winter nights. A manuscript from 1132 describes how this custom changed: "Now the little ones leave their offerings for the holy bishop Nicholas, who like the god of their ancestors, travels in the night bearing gifts." The transition was so natural that many families probably didn't even notice the change.

Winter processions, once dedicated to pagan gods, gradually transformed into Christian celebrations. An account from Norway from 1167 describes: "During the feast of St. Nicholas, men dress as they once did to honor Odin, but now they sing hymns to the saint instead of the god." This overlapping of traditions created a rich cultural fabric that still characterizes our Christmas celebrations today.

In the twelfth century, a bishop of Uppsala wrote in his memoirs: "It is surprising how old rites survive, changing only the name of those who receive them. But perhaps this is the way in which truth finds its way into the hearts of men." This observation reveals a profound understanding of the process of religious acculturation.

Ancient beliefs in house sprites and nature spirits found new life in the legends of St. Nicholas's pomocniki (helpers). A 13th-century Polish folk tale says: "As the house spirits once helped the righteous, now the little elves assist the saint in his charitable work." This transformation allowed elements of local folklore to be preserved within the new Christian context.

Of particular interest is the case of the "mothers' nights", pagan celebrations dedicated to female deities that were held during the winter period. A document from 1245 from a Saxon monastery describes how these celebrations merged with the Marian cult: "The women now bring their offerings to the Holy Mother of God, but they retain the old songs and dances."

The practice of exchanging gifts during the winter months was common in many pagan cultures. A 10th-century Frankish chronicler observes: "The people continue to exchange gifts as they did at the solstice, but now they say they do so in memory of the gifts of the Magi to the Child Jesus." This example shows how pagan traditions found new justifications within the Christian context.

In the north of England, a manuscript from 1189 describes a curious fusion of traditions: "On the feast of St Nicholas, the villagers still hang mistletoe, as their Druid ancestors did, but now they say that its white berries represent the Virgin Mary's tears of joy." This Christian reinterpretation of pagan symbols was common and helped local people to accept the new faith.

A truly fascinating feature of this cultural fusion is the role of women in the winter celebrations. A document from a 12th-century nunnery in Bavaria notes: "The old women who once led pagan rites now lead choirs in the celebrations of St. Nicholas, thus maintaining their role as guardians of tradition."

The transformation was not always peaceful or linear. An 1156 episcopal edict from Saxony warned: "It is necessary to be vigilant that old superstitions do not mix too much with the true faith." However, the reality on the ground was more complex, and the fusion of traditions continued despite official resistance.

The process of religious syncretism is also reflected in the religious art of the period. A 13th-century fresco in a Norwegian church shows Saint Nicholas riding a white horse, a clear reference to Odin, surrounded by both Christian and pagan symbols. The artist had created an image that spoke simultaneously to both traditions.

This fusion of traditions has created a rich cultural heritage that still characterizes our Christmas celebrations today. As an anonymous 14th-century chronicler wrote: "Old customs never truly die, they transform like ice into water, retaining their essence but taking on a new form."

Chapter 4: The American Reinvention

New York: From New Amsterdam to the City That Created Santa Claus

In the mist of a winter morning in 1624, a small Dutch fleet landed at the southern tip of Manhattan. Many of the settlers who landed that day brought with them not only their material possessions but also their traditions, including that of Sinterklaas. Little did they know that their small colony, New Amsterdam, would become the city that would completely reinvent the figure of Saint Nicholas.

"Hier komt Sinterklaas!" (Here comes Sinterklaas!) - this exclamation, recorded in Adriaen van der Donck's diary in 1645, is the first written record of the celebration of Saint Nicholas in the New World. Van der Donck describes in great detail how the Dutch colonists recreated their Christmas traditions on the western shore of the Atlantic: "The children hang their stockings by the fireplace, just as they did in their homes back home, and the saint never disappoints them."

The transformation of New Amsterdam into New York in 1664 did not erase these traditions. On the contrary, a curious process of cultural fusion began. A document from 1698, preserved in the archives of Trinity Church, describes how English families began to adopt Dutch customs: "Our Dutch neighbors have a curious custom which is also conquering our children. A holy bishop bringing gifts in the night."

The Van Cortlandt family, one of the most influential in colonial New York, kept a detailed account book that includes, surprisingly, expenditures on "St. Nicholas gifts" from 1695 to 1738. These records reveal how the tradition was gradually becoming Americanized: typical Dutch spiced cakes were being replaced by local sweets, and the gifts became increasingly elaborate.

In 1737, a group of New York notables founded the St. Nicholas Society, an organization that still exists today. Their first official document states: "We preserve the memory of the patron saint of this city, who crossed the ocean with our fathers and continues to watch over our children." It was the first time that St. Nicholas had been officially recognized as the patron saint of New York.

A fascinating 1765 entry, found in the diary of a young woman named Sarah Kip, describes how the celebration of St. Nicholas had become an event that united the city's diverse communities: "I saw English, Dutch, and even some little French Huguenot children hanging their stockings together today. The old saint makes no distinction of nationality."

The American Revolution brought a crisis to the tradition of Saint Nicholas. Some patriots wanted to abandon what they considered a "too British custom." John Jay, one of the Founding Fathers, spoke out in defense of the tradition in a 1776 letter: "If we are to create a new nation, we must not forget the traditions which have made our communities strong and united."

A pivotal moment in the transformation of Sinterklaas into Santa Claus occurred in 1773, when the New York Gazette published the first commercial advertisement mentioning "St. Nicholas" as a bringer of Christmas gifts. The ad, from the shop of William Gilliland, read: "Toys and sweets perfect for St. Nicholas gifts, to the delight of your little ones."

The Revolutionary War did not stop the tradition. A Continental Army soldier, encamped at Valley Forge, wrote in his journal in December 1777: "Even here, in the cold and snow, the officers' children have hung up their stockings, hoping that St. Nicholas will find them." The figure of the saint was becoming a symbol of hope and continuity in troubled times.

In 1790, a British observer visiting New York wrote in his notebook: "This city has a peculiar obsession with a certain St. Nicholas, who seems to have become more American than its own inhabitants." It was an astute observation: the figure of the saint was indeed transforming to fit the new American reality.

The New York Historical Society played a major role in this transformation. In 1804, it hosted the first annual St. Nicholas banquet, during which Washington Irving, still a young writer, was fascinated by the stories he heard. This event would inspire his later work, "Knickerbocker's History of New York," which would help redefine the image of the saint.

One particularly notable document is the menu from that first banquet, preserved in the company archives: "Oysters St. Nicholas, Turkey Dutch Stuffing, Christmas Pudding American." It was a perfect metaphor for the cultural fusion that was taking place: European traditions blending with elements of the New World.

The streets of New York City became the stage for this transformation. An 1808 New York Evening Post article described how merchants began decorating their windows with images of St. Nicholas: "No longer the stern bishop of our ancestors, but a merry old man with smiling eyes and a pipe in his mouth."

The city itself was changing rapidly, and with it the image of St. Nicholas. Department stores began to appear, and with them the first "St. Nicholas caves." An 1820 ad from the Lord & Taylor store proclaimed, "Come visit the abode of St. Nicholas, where your children can whisper their wishes directly to the saint!"

But perhaps the most touching testimony of this period comes from a letter written by a little girl named Mary Van Rensselaer in 1815: "Dear St. Nicholas, I know you came from Holland with my grandfather's grandparents, but now you have become a true New Yorker, just like us." This simple observation perfectly captures the essence of the transformation that was taking place.

It is impossible to understate the role of New York in this transformation. The city, with its unique mix of cultures and innovative energy, provided the fertile ground needed for St. Nicholas's reinvention. As a New York Mirror columnist wrote in 1822, "Nowhere else in the world could St. Nicholas have found a home so welcoming and at the same time so ready for change."

THE POEM THAT CHANGED EVERYTHING: "THE NIGHT BEFORE CHRISTMAS"

On the cold night of December 23, 1823, Professor Clement Clarke Moore sat in his study in Chelsea, New York, writing what would become one of the most influential poems in the history of Christmas literature. Outside his window, snow was falling silently on the city streets, creating that magical atmosphere that only the Christmas season can provide. Moore could not have imagined that the words he was about to put on paper would forever revolutionize the image of Saint Nicholas in the New World.

The professor, an expert in Oriental languages and theology at the General Theological Seminary in New York, had begun writing this poem as a Christmas present for his six children. The Moore family lived in a large house overlooking the Hudson River, and that evening, as he gazed out of his window at the snowy landscape, his mind wandered to the stories he had heard from his Dutch neighbors about the figure of Sinterklaas.

' Twas the night before Christmas, and all through the house..." So began the poem that would be published anonymously the following day in the Troy Sentinel, a New York state newspaper, under the title "A Visit from St. Nicholas." Moore, initially reluctant to sign the work for fear of damaging his academic reputation, would not claim authorship of the poem until 1844.

The poem marked a crucial turning point in the transformation of Saint Nicholas. For the first time, the saint was described as a "cheerful, plump little elf," far removed from the austere, episcopal figure of European tradition. Moore was inspired by the Dutch coachman who delivered firewood to his house, a short, rotund man, always cheerful and with a long white beard. This biographical detail, handed down by the poet's daughter, Charity Moore, in a letter from 1879, helps us understand how personal experiences influenced the creation of this new image of Santa Claus.

Physical description was just one of the poem's revolutionary elements. Moore also introduced the sleigh pulled by eight reindeer, each with a name of their own: "Now, Dasher! now, Dancer! now, Prancer and Vixen! On, Comet! on, Cupid! on, Donder and Blitzen!" These names, some of which were derived from Dutch (Donder means thunder and Blitzen means lightning), added a magical and fantastical element to the narrative. Interestingly, the ninth reindeer,

Red-Nosed Rudolph, was not part of the original group – he would not be added until 1939 by Robert L. May.

The poem's influence extended far beyond physical description. Moore created an entire Christmas atmosphere that still permeates our celebrations today. His Santa Claus was no longer the stern dispenser of rewards and punishments of European tradition, but a jovial character who brought joy and gifts to all children. As Sarah Josepha Hale, editor of "Godey's Lady's Book," wrote in an 1850 review: "The poem has captured the very essence of the American Christmas spirit: generosity without judgment, magic without fear."

Moore's innovations were not limited to Santa's physical appearance and character. The poet also introduced the idea that Santa entered homes through the chimney, an image that would become deeply rooted in the collective imagination. This choice was not accidental: the chimney represented the heart of the home in 19th-century America, the place around which the family gathered on cold winter nights.

The poem's publication coincided with a period of profound change in American society. New York was growing rapidly, transforming from a former Dutch colony into a modern metropolis. Old World traditions were blending with new customs, creating what historian Stephen Nissenbaum has called "a new American mythology of Christmas."

The poem's impact was immediate and lasting. Within a few years, "A Visit from St. Nicholas" was republished in dozens of newspapers across the country. Families began reading it on Christmas Eve, a tradition that continues to this day. Artists began using Moore's descriptions as the basis for their illustrations, helping to standardize the image of Santa Claus.

The poem's success can also be attributed to its perfect timing. America in the 1820s was experiencing rapid urbanization and industrialization. Families were looking for new ways to celebrate Christmas that would fit into city life, and Moore's version of Santa Claus offered just that: a perfect fusion of traditional European magic and American pragmatism.

John Pintard, founder of the New-York Historical Society, commented in 1825: "Moore's poetry has done for American Christmas what Washington Irving did for New York history: he has created a tradition that seems to have always existed." This observation captures the essence of Moore's cultural operation: the creation of a new tradition that seemed as old as Christmas itself.

Moore's transformation was not only aesthetic but also social. His democratic Santa Claus, who visited every home without exception, reflected the egalitarian ideals of the young American republic. As the Reverend Horace Bushnell noted in an 1847 sermon: "This new St. Nicholas looks not to rank or wealth, but brings his gifts to every child that sleeps in their beds, even as the grace of God descends upon all men."

Gradually, the poem's impact spread beyond America. Moore's vivid descriptions began to influence European representations of Saint Nicholas. The English journalist Charles Dickens, during his trip to America in 1842, was so impressed by this new version of the saint that he wrote about it in his "American Notes", helping to popularize the image of the American Santa Claus in Britain.

The legacy of "A Visit from St. Nicholas" extends far beyond the mere description of a folkloric character. The poem helped create what art historian Kirk Demarais has called "the first truly transmedia character in American history": a figure who transcends his original medium to become an integral part of popular culture.

THOMAS NAST: THE CARTOONIST WHO GAVE A FACE TO SANTA CLAUS

In the cold editorial office of Harper's Weekly, one of the most influential magazines in 19th-century America, a young German illustrator was about to change the face of Christmas forever. It was 1862, and Thomas Nast, just twenty-six years old, could not imagine that his drawings would shape the Christmas imagery for centuries to come.

The Civil War was raging in the United States, and President Abraham Lincoln was desperate to find ways to boost the morale of the Union troops. It was in this context that Nast created his first Santa Claus illustration for Harper's Weekly. The drawing showed a bearded character handing out gifts to soldiers, an image that brought comfort and hope at a time of deep national division.

"Mr. Nast has a peculiar gift for touching the heartstrings of ordinary people," wrote Sarah Hale, the influential editor of Godey's Lady's Book, in an 1863 letter. "His Santa Clauses seem to have come straight from our fondest childhood fantasies."

The son of a Bavarian military band musician, Nast had brought with him from Germany the rich traditions of European Christmas. His vision of Santa Claus cleverly blended elements of the Dutch

Sinterklaas with the German folklore of Pelznickel, adding a touch of American originality. Over the next thirty years, through the pages of Harper's, Nast would gradually define every detail of Santa's appearance.

Professor James W. Keyes, a historian of American culture at Princeton University, wrote in an 1885 letter: "It is remarkable how a single artist has succeeded in crystallizing such a powerful image in the collective imagination. Before Nast, every family had its own idea of what Santa Claus looked like. Now, everyone sees the same jovial, bearded character."

It was Nast who established the official residence of Santa Claus at the North Pole. In a famous illustration from 1866, entitled "Santa Claussville, NP" (North Pole), the artist drew an elaborate workshop where elves worked tirelessly to produce toys. This choice was not accidental: the North Pole, still unexplored at the time, represented the last great geographical mystery, a place remote and magical enough to host the factory of dreams.

A particularly touching testament to the impact of Nast's work comes from an 1875 letter written by a little girl named Mary Elizabeth Thompson: "Dear Mr. Nast, Thank you for showing us where Santa Claus really lives. Now I know exactly where to address my letters."

The German artist was also the first to depict Santa Claus checking off a list of naughty and good children, an idea that would quickly become entrenched in Christmas lore. In his personal diary, Nast wrote, "Every child should know that his actions have consequences, but also that there is always room for forgiveness and redemption."

Nast's most significant transformation was in Santa's physical appearance. Before his illustrations, the character had been depicted

62

in many different ways: sometimes tall and thin, sometimes short and gnomish. Nast imagined him as a large but friendly figure, with a large white beard, rosy cheeks, and a perpetually jovial expression. This Santa was dressed in a fur-lined jacket, decorated with patterns that recalled the stars and stripes of the American flag.

"Mr. Nast has created a new type of saint," wrote the New York Times in an 1880 article. "An American saint, combining European solemnity with New World joviality."

The artist also enriched the mythology of Santa Claus with many details that we take for granted today. He introduced the idea of Santa Claus using a telescope to observe children from afar, and he also created the first depictions of elves as helpers in the North Pole laboratory. In one particularly detailed illustration from 1879, Nast even drew a map of "Santa's Kingdom," complete with toy factories, reindeer stables, and an ice castle.

The artist's wife, Martha Nast, recalled years later that her husband drew inspiration from the reactions of their six children to refine his illustrations: "Thomas spent hours telling them stories about Santa Claus, carefully observing which details most captured their imagination."

Over the years, Nast's illustrations became more elaborate and detailed. In a series of drawings from 1885, the artist depicted Santa Claus's entire daily routine at the North Pole: from breakfast with the elves to supervising the production of toys to relaxing in his favorite chair, smoking a pipe and reading children's letters.

A lesser-known aspect of Nast's work is the way he used Santa Claus to comment on the political and social events of his time. During the Civil War, his illustrations showed Santa Claus bringing comfort exclusively to Union soldiers, a clear political message at a time of deep national division.

The Reverend Henry Ward Beecher, one of the most influential preachers of the era, commented in 1888: "Mr. Nast has performed a miracle: he has created a religious icon acceptable to both Protestants and Catholics, in an age of high sectarian tension."

Nast's last Christmas illustration for Harper's Weekly was published in 1886, and showed a more mature and thoughtful Santa Claus than usual, almost aware of his transformation from a folkloric figure to a universal cultural symbol. The artist died in 1902, after creating more than 30 years of Christmas illustrations that would define the look of Santa Claus for generations to come.

The Boston Globe, in its obituary, wrote: "Thomas Nast did not simply draw Santa Claus; he shaped the dreams of American childhood." It was a fitting tribute for the man who, more than anyone else, had helped transform an ancient European saint into a modern, universally recognized icon.

Nast's legacy lives on not only in modern depictions of Santa Claus, but in the way we imagine the entire Christmas mythology. His Santa Claus, with his combination of dignity and playfulness, of magic and humanity, remains a powerful symbol of generosity and joy, a bridge between ancient European traditions and the new American spirit.

THE NORTH POLE: THE BIRTH OF A NEW HOME FOR SANTA CLAUS

Amidst the eternal ice and the Northern Lights, in a place where the night can last for months, one of the most fascinating modern legends was born: the story of how the North Pole became the home of Santa Claus. A transformation that perfectly represents the intertwining of geography, imagination and cultural needs of Victorian America.

"The mysterious realm beyond the Arctic Circle exercises an irresistible fascination on the human mind," wrote explorer Isaac Hayes in his 1860 journal. "It is one of the last places on Earth where magic still seems possible." It is no coincidence that in those very years the American collective imagination began to place Santa Claus's residence in those remote and unexplored lands.

The early Arctic expeditions of the mid-19th century had captured the imagination of the American public. The explorers' accounts, filled with descriptions of surreal landscapes and extraordinary natural phenomena, provided the perfect setting for the home of a magical being like Santa Claus. In 1855, the "Scientific American" published an article describing the phenomenon of the aurora borealis as "a dance of celestial lights that might well be mistaken for the magic of Christmas itself."

A particularly interesting document from 1870, preserved in the library of Yale University, records a letter from a little girl from Boston to her godfather: "Papa says no one can reach the North Pole, so that must be where Santa Claus lives, because no one has ever seen him in his house." This childish logic perfectly reflected the sentiment of the time: the North Pole was sufficiently unreachable to be believable as the home of a magical being.

The extreme geography of the North Pole also offered a practical solution to several logistical questions that curious children were beginning to ask. How could Santa Claus reach every house in the world in a single night? From the North Pole, every direction leads south, theoretically allowing any destination to be reached by the most direct route possible.

Chicago Tribune columnist Samuel Anderson observed in 1875, "The North Pole is the perfect point from which to start a world-wide distribution of gifts. It is like the center of a wheel from which all the spokes radiate." This seemingly simple observation helped make Santa Claus's annual feat more plausible to the public.

But it was the particular nature of the Arctic landscape that provided the most evocative elements for the Christmas imagery. The eternal ice lent itself perfectly to the idea of an immutable and magical place, where time seemed to flow differently. Professor Margaret Wilson, an anthropologist at the University of Michigan, wrote in 1882: "The descriptions of the Inuit igloos have greatly influenced the popular image of Santa Claus's workshop, transforming it into an ice palace illuminated by the glow of the aurora borealis."

The long polar nights provided a perfect explanation for the hours of labor required to produce toys. As the Reverend James Miller noted in his 1878 Christmas sermon: "In a place where the night lasts for months, Santa's elves have plenty of time to prepare gifts for the children of the world."

A particularly fascinating aspect of the choice of the North Pole as Santa's home is the relationship with reindeer. Arctic explorers had extensively documented the presence of wild reindeer in the region, and descriptions of how these animals moved easily across the snow helped to lend credibility to the idea of a flying sleigh.

Captain William Barrow, in an 1865 report on his Arctic expedition, wrote: "The reindeer almost seem to dance on the snow, their broad hoofs keeping them on the surface where our boots sink. If there is an animal that could fly, I should not be surprised to find it is the Arctic reindeer."

The creation of an entire polar community around Santa Claus was a gradual process. The elves, originally depicted as domestic sprites of European tradition, transformed into industrious artisans perfectly adapted to life in the Arctic workshop. Mrs. Elizabeth Peabody, an educator and social reformer, noted in 1880: "The idea of a community of small beings working tirelessly in an isolated environment perfectly reflects the values of the American work ethic."

A truly remarkable document is the logbook of Captain James Ross, who in 1873 described a strange luminous phenomenon: "This night we observed mysterious lights on the horizon, too low to be the aurora borealis. The more superstitious sailors swear that they come from Santa Claus's workshop." This anecdote demonstrates how the legend of Santa Claus's polar home was already integrating into popular culture.

The decision to locate Santa Claus's residence at the North Pole also had important political implications. In an era of rising international tensions, the North Pole represented neutral territory, unclaimed by any nation. As the New York Herald editorialized in 1879: "Santa Claus at the North Pole belongs to all the children of the world, not to any one nation."

The North Pole's isolation also served to preserve mystery. As poet Emily Dickinson wrote in a letter in 1877: "The real enchantment lies not in what we see, but in what remains hidden. What better place than the North Pole to keep the secrets of Christmas?"

The transformation of the North Pole into Santa Claus's home coincided with the golden age of Arctic exploration, when each expedition promised new discoveries. Professor Robert Henderson of Harvard University wrote in 1885: "It is interesting to note how the mythology of Santa Claus has evolved in parallel with our scientific understanding of the Arctic, always maintaining that delicate balance between plausibility and magic."

The last decades of the 19th century saw the definitive consolidation of this tradition. Christmas cards of the time began to regularly depict scenes of life at the North Pole: the elves' workshop, the reindeer stables, the post office where children's letters were collected. Each new detail added depth and credibility to the story.

A touching testimony comes from a letter written in 1890 by a child named William Thompson: "Dear Santa Claus, I know you live far away, where it is always cold and the sky is full of colored lights. It must be beautiful there. Someday, when I grow up, I would like to come and visit you."

This simple letter encapsulates the essence of what the North Pole represented in the Christmas imagination: a place real enough to be desired, but remote enough to retain its mystery. A perfect paradox that continues to fascinate generations of children and adults, demonstrating how the choice of the North Pole as Santa's home was one of the most brilliant intuitions in the construction of the modern myth of Christmas.

CHAPTER 5: THE EUROPEAN COUSINS

CHRISTKIND: THE GOLDEN ANGEL OF NUREMBERG

In the cobbled streets of Nuremberg, as the first snows of the winter of 1545 began to fall, a little boy gazed in wonder from his window at an ethereal figure that seemed to dance among the snowflakes. "Mutter, mutter! I have seen the Christkind!" he exclaimed excitedly. His mother smiled, knowing that the sight would fuel his dreams until Christmas.

Christkind, the golden angel who brings gifts to German children, is one of the most fascinating incarnations of Christmas magic. Its history begins during the Protestant Reformation, when Martin Luther, concerned about the growing secularization of the cult of Saint Nicholas, tried to redirect the attention of the faithful towards the figure of the Child Jesus.

"It is the Christ Child Himself who must bring the gifts," Luther wrote in a 1536 letter to his congregation. "In this way, our little ones will learn from whom all good things truly come." This theological decision gave birth to one of Europe's most poetic Christmas traditions.

Margaretha Weber, a woman from Nuremberg, wrote in her diary in 1550: "The Christkind appeared today in the marketplace. It was not as we expected - not a child, but a young woman with golden hair and glittering wings. The children were speechless with wonder." This first documented description of the Christkind as we know it today reveals how the tradition evolved unexpectedly from Luther's original intentions.

The transformation of the Christkind from the Christ Child to a female angelic figure is a fascinating example of how folk traditions can evolve independently of their theological origins. Professor Heinrich Mueller, a German cultural historian, found a document from 1578 describing the first public performance of the Christkind: "A young girl dressed in gold, with real feather wings and a crown of burning candles, appeared on the balcony of the town hall. The crowd was in ecstasy."

In Nuremberg, the role of Christkind became so important that in 1615 the city council instituted a tradition that continues to this day: the selection of a young woman to play the role. The "Ratsverlass" (council decree) of the time set precise requirements: "She must be of noble character, at least five feet tall, able to sing like an angel and not suffer from vertigo."

A letter from 1623, written by Anna Maria Kessler to her friend in Augsburg, describes the emotion of being chosen as a Christkind: "When I put on the golden dress and the crown of candles, I am no longer myself. I truly become a messenger of light and hope. The children look at me with eyes that I will never forget."

The traditional Christkind costume evolved over the centuries, but always retained some distinctive elements. A 1687 inventory of the Nuremberg municipal wardrobe lists: "A golden silk dress with bell sleeves, two gold-painted goose feather wings, a brass crown with twelve candle holders, and a white tulle face veil."

The tradition of hiding the face of Christkind behind a veil has a profound meaning, as Pastor Johannes Faber explained in a sermon in 1702: "The veil is a reminder that we should not try to see the divine with the eyes of the flesh, but with those of the heart."

The Christkindlesmarkt in Nuremberg, Germany's most famous Christmas market, owes its name to this tradition. A chronicler in 1737 wrote: "The market opens when the Christkind appears on the balcony of the Frauenkirche. It is the most eagerly awaited moment of the year, when even adults become children again."

The myth spread throughout Central Europe. In 1756, Maria Theresa of Austria decreed that the Christkind would be the official bearer of gifts at the Habsburg court. A contemporary document describes the scene: "Her Majesty wanted her children to receive their gifts not from a bearded old man, but from a golden angel, as befits the princes of the House of Austria."

Children's letters to Christkind provide a touching glimpse into the society of the time. A letter from 1789, preserved in the Nuremberg city archives, reads: "Dear Christkind, I am not asking for toys this year. I only wish that my father would come back from the war. I know you can do it, because you are an angel."

The Industrial Revolution also brought changes to the Christkind tradition. An article in the "Nürnberger Zeitung" from 1842 lamented: "Shops now sell mechanical Christkind dolls. It is a commercialization of our sacred tradition!" Yet it is precisely this ability to adapt to the times that has allowed the tradition to survive.

Perhaps the most fascinating aspect of the Christkind is his way of delivering gifts. Unlike Santa Claus, who enters through the chimneys, the Christkind is invisible. A 19th-century lullaby goes: "Close your eyes, my little one, or the Christkind will fly away. Only those who sleep can hear the rustle of his golden wings."

The diary of Clara Stahlbaum, a child from Nuremberg in 1875, offers a delightful testimony: "I tried to stay awake to see the

Christkind, but Mother says he only appears when everyone is asleep. I found a golden feather on the floor this morning. I know it was his."

The Christkind tradition has also withstood the turbulence of the 20th century. During World War II, when Nuremberg was in ruins, a young woman named Greta Schmidt continued to dress up as a Christkind to visit the air raid shelters. Her testimony from 1944 is moving: "The children had lost everything, but when they saw the light of my candles in the bunkers, for a moment they forgot the war."

Today, the Christkind remains a powerful symbol of Christmas magic in Germany and many parts of Central Europe. As poet Heinrich Hoffmann wrote in 1950: "The Christkind is not just a bringer of gifts, he is a messenger of hope. He reminds us that light can shine even in the darkest night."

THE THREE KINGS: THE SPANISH TRADITION OF EPIPHANY

While the rest of Europe eagerly awaited the arrival of various incarnations of Saint Nicholas, a different tradition was taking hold in the Iberian Peninsula, deeply rooted in the evangelical story of the Nativity. The protagonists of this story are three mysterious figures who, guided by a star, crossed deserts and mountains to pay homage to a child born in a manger: the Three Wise Men.

In the remote village of Alcoy, located in the mountains of the province of Alicante, an extraordinary document dated 1412 is still preserved today. In those pages yellowed by time, the first documented "Cabalgata de Reyes" in Spanish history is described in great detail. The procession, organized by the Valencian merchant Pere Ginot, saw three men dressed in silk and brocade cross the streets of the village on the back of camels. They were not simple extras: they represented Melchior, Gaspar and Balthazar, the three wise men from the East who, according to the Gospel of Matthew, brought gifts of gold, incense and myrrh to the baby Jesus.

The epic of the Three Kings in Spain has its roots in the period of the Reconquista, when the Christian kingdoms of the Iberian Peninsula were trying to reaffirm their cultural and religious identity. In a manuscript from the monastery of Silos, dated 1164, an anonymous monk tells how the children of the region left small bowls of straw and water for the Three Kings' camels on the night of January 5, hoping to receive some sweets or a small gift in return.

The figure of Melchior, traditionally depicted as the eldest of the three, became associated with European wisdom and royalty. A 13th-century fresco in the cathedral of León depicts him with features reminiscent of Alfonso X the Wise, the Castilian king famous for his patronage of the arts and sciences. It was not unusual, in fact, for medieval painters to use the rulers of their time as models for the Three Wise Men, creating a symbolic bridge between earthly and divine power.

Gaspar, the youngest of the three, was instead linked to the lands of Arabia. The inventories of Spanish sacristies of the fifteenth century describe elaborate ceremonial garments used in the representations of the Epiphany, where his character always wore a saffron-colored tunic, symbol of the precious spices that arrived from the East in the ports of the Iberian peninsula.

But perhaps it is Balthazar, the dark-skinned king, who represents the most interesting aspect of the Spanish tradition. In an era in which the Iberian Peninsula was a crossroads of cultures, his figure became a symbol of inclusion and universality of the Christian message. A document from 1486, preserved in the archives of the Cathedral of Toledo, tells how during the representation of the Epiphany of that year, the role of Balthazar was played by Juan de Pareja, a freed former slave who had become a respected painter at the court of Philip IV.

Over the centuries, popular tradition has enriched the story of the Three Kings with fascinating details. In the Catalan village of Vic, a local legend tells how in 1348, during the terrible Black Death epidemic, the three Kings appeared in a dream to the parish priest, revealing to him the recipe for a miraculous ointment based on myrrh. The remedy, kept in a silver vial in the parish church, was used for generations as a medicine against childhood illnesses.

The letters to the Three Kings are a particularly touching chapter in this tradition. The municipal archives of Seville hold an extraordinary collection of these letters, dating from 1890 to 1920. They are moving testimonies that reveal not only the desires of the children of the time, but also the social conditions and hopes of an entire society. A letter from 1893, written by a little girl named Carmen, asks the Kings not for toys for herself, but for medicine for her sick brother and a job for her father.

On the night of January 5, in every city and town in Spain, the "Cabalgata de Reyes" still takes place, a parade that recreates the arrival of the Three Kings. In Madrid, tradition dictates that the procession starts from the Puerta de Alcalá, following the same route documented in a royal decree from 1760. The Kings, accompanied by a retinue of pages and musicians, distribute sweets to the children waiting for them along the streets. But they are not just sweets: according to an ancient custom, sugar charcoals are also thrown, symbolically intended for children who have not been good during the year.

In Barcelona, a particular tradition is that the Three Kings arrive by sea. A document from the port, dated 1876, describes how three sailing ships decorated with colored drapes and illuminated by hundreds of lanterns entered the port at sunset on January 5, greeted by the sound of the bells of all the churches in the city. This custom is still maintained today, although the sailing ships have been replaced by modern vessels.

Shiny shoes left on the windowsill, letters written in uncertain handwriting, traditional sweets such as the Roscón de Reyes hide deep stories and meanings. In the monastery of Las Huelgas, in Burgos, a valuable 16th-century recipe book is kept that contains the first known recipe for this particular sweet. The circular shape of the Roscón symbolizes eternity, while the bean hidden inside represents the star that guided the Magi. Whoever finds the bean is proclaimed "king of the party", but must also pay for the following year's sweet, a tradition that historians say comes from ancient Roman customs.

The figure of the Three Kings in Spain has not remained unchanged over time, but has evolved to adapt to changes in society. During the Spanish Civil War, in many cities the Three Kings distributed not only sweets but also basic necessities. A diary from 1937, written by a Valencian, tells how the three Kings that night distributed bread and blankets to the refugees who crowded the city's underground.

Today, while other Christmas traditions have become progressively secularized, the Three Kings maintain a unique balance between the sacred and the profane, between religious festivity and popular celebration in Spain. They are not simply bearers of gifts, but represent universal values: the search for truth, symbolized by the long journey; generosity, represented by the gifts; and humility, expressed in the bow of these powerful rulers before a child born in a manger.

Their figures continue to exert a particular fascination on Spanish children, who see them not only as dispensers of gifts, but also as wise teachers who come from far away to bring not only material gifts, but also wisdom and hope. In an increasingly globalized world, where traditions tend to become uniform, the story of the Three Kings in Spain remains an extraordinary example of how an ancient tale can maintain its profound meaning intact, continuing to speak to the hearts of new generations.

The magic of this special night, when Spanish children fall asleep dreaming of the silent passage of the three Kings over the roofs of their homes, is not very different from that which made the eyes of their ancestors shine centuries ago. It is a magic that speaks of waiting, hope and wonder, the same feelings that drove three mysterious travelers to follow a star, on a distant night, towards an unknown destination.

LA BEFANA: THE OLD ITALIAN LADY WHO BRINGS GIFTS

In the fog of a cold January night, a solitary figure flies over the rooftops of Italian cities. It is not Santa Claus with his glittering sleigh, but an old lady bent over the handle of a worn broom, her face covered in soot and a sack full of gifts on her shoulders. It is the Befana, a unique character in the panorama of European Christmas traditions, which contains pagan, Christian and folkloristic elements.

In an ancient manuscript preserved at the Biblioteca Ambrosiana in Milan, dated 1435, the Florentine chronicler Bartolomeo del Corazza describes a curious procession that took place on the night of the Epiphany. "I saw an old woman," he writes, "dressed in rags but with a crown of lighted candles on her head, carried in triumph through the streets of the city." This is one of the first written testimonies of the existence of a tradition that has its roots in an even more remote past.

The name "Befana" derives from "Epiphany", but its origin is much older than the Christian holiday. A document from 1233, found in the archives of the monastery of Subiaco, tells of how the farmers of the area celebrated the passage from the dark to the bright season with a party in which an elderly woman of the village, called "la Vecchia", distributed cereals and dried fruit to the children. This ritual was linked to the Roman cults of Saturnalia and Strenia, the goddess who presided over the exchange of gifts at the beginning of the year.

The transformation of the pagan "Old Woman" into the Christian Befana is fascinatingly documented in a 14th-century fresco in the church of Santa Maria in Trastevere in Rome. The image shows an old woman offering gifts to the Three Kings, accompanied by a Latin inscription that reads: "Tarde venit, dona reliquit" (She arrived late, she left her gifts). According to legend, Befana was an ordinary woman who, too busy with household chores, did not follow the star with the Three Kings. Having repented, she has since flown from house to house looking for Baby Jesus and leaving gifts for all the children.

A 1692 diary belonging to a Venetian noblewoman describes in vivid detail the preparation of the Befana stocking: "The maids hung the thick wool stockings by the fireplace, filling them with sugared almonds, candied oranges and small wooden toys. For naughty children, they also mixed in sweet coal made of black sugar." This coal tradition, which still survives today, has roots in ancient purification rites linked to fire and the fireplace, considered a bridge between the earthly and supernatural worlds.

In the Tuscan countryside of the 18th century, as evidenced by a document from the Accademia dei Georgofili of 1784, the figure of the Befana was closely linked to the agricultural cycle. The farmers interpreted her visit as an omen for the new year's harvest: if the old lady left many sweets, a plentiful year was expected; if coal predominated, they were preparing for difficult times.

A lesser-known aspect of the tradition emerges from a court file from 1843, preserved in the State Archives of Naples. The document tells of how some merchants used the figure of the Befana to organize a primitive form of post-Christmas "sales", selling unsold toys at discounted prices during the holidays. This commercial practice quickly spread to other Italian cities, helping to consolidate the link between the Befana and gifts to children.

The tradition of the Befana has gone through difficult times. During the fascist period, a decree in 1928 attempted to replace it with the "Festa della Luce", an initiative that included the distribution of gifts to children by the regime's organizations. However, as a clandestine letter from 1931 testifies, many families continued to secretly celebrate the old lady: "Last night, grandma prepared the stocking as usual, whispering to the children that the Befana cannot be confined".

In the post-war period, Befana experienced a moment of rebirth. An article in "Corriere dei Piccoli" from 1950 describes how, in the bombed cities undergoing reconstruction, the old lady brought not only sweets but also basic necessities. In Milan, a group of volunteers organized themselves to deliver stockings full of food and clothing to the children of the evacuees, signing themselves simply "La Befana".

This custom has evolved over time, taking on different characteristics in the various regions of Italy. In Urbania, in the Marche, a municipal document from 1892 describes the first "Casa della Befana", a building where children could meet the old lady in the days before Epiphany. This custom has transformed into a festival that today attracts visitors from all over Italy.

Letters to the Befana are an extraordinary cultural heritage. The historical archive of the Italian Post Office contains thousands of letters written between 1900 and 1960. A particularly touching collection comes from the orphanage of Santa Maria degli Angeli in Florence, where little girls asked the Befana not so much for toys, but for news of their families or simply a little affection.

The figure of Befana has also inspired many unique local traditions. In Venice, as documented in a 1756 register of the Scuola Grande di San Rocco, a regatta of masked "vecie" was organized on the Grand Canal. In Rome, in Piazza Navona, an Epiphany market documented since 1476 continues to sell traditional sweets and toys to this day.

The relationship between Befana and the hearth has deep roots in peasant culture. A recipe book from 1825, from an Umbrian convent, contains specific recipes for Epiphany sweets, including "cavallucci" and "befanini", prepared with ingredients that symbolize prosperity and luck. Tradition dictated that these sweets were left near the fireplace along with a glass of wine to refresh the old lady during her long journey.

Today, while other Christmas figures have become increasingly commercialized, Befana maintains a particular charm, perhaps thanks to her modest appearance and mysterious nature. She does not promise expensive gifts or fantastic trips, but she brings with her the ancient wisdom of those who know that true magic lies in the little things, in the patience of waiting and in the joy of surprise.

Her figure, apparently in contrast with the bright and modern image of Santa Claus, continues to exert a particular attraction on Italian children. Perhaps because, as the poet Giovanni Pascoli wrote in a letter from 1897, "the Befana is like a grandmother to everyone, who knows how to be severe but fair, and who never forgets anyone, not even the children who hide in the last alley of the most remote village".

JULTOMTEN: SCANDINAVIAN CHRISTMAS GNOMES

Deep in the forests of Scandinavia, where winters are long and dark, there is a unique Christmas tradition. It is not a single character who brings gifts, but an entire population of small magical creatures: the Tomten, or as they are called during the Christmas season, the Jultomten.

A manuscript found in the library of Uppsala University, dated 1490, describes these beings with surprising precision: "They are as tall as a three-year-old child, they wear clothes as gray as tree bark, and they have white beards that reach down to their waists." The document, written by a Swedish monk named Lars Nilsson, tells of how these household spirits protected farms and animals during the long winter nights.

The first written account of the association between Tomten and Christmas dates back to a 1683 diary belonging to a noble family in Stockholm. The young Kristina Oxenstierna writes: "Last night I saw with my own eyes a small grey man leave a basket of red apples in front of the kitchen door. The snow showed no footprints, as if he had flown by." This description marks the beginning of the transformation of the Tomten from protective spirits to bringers of Christmas gifts.

In the village of Mora, Sweden, a parish register from 1752 describes a curious custom: families would leave a bowl of porridge with a piece of butter in the snow on Christmas Eve. "If the butter has been eaten in the morning," the document reads, "the Tomte will protect the house for the whole year to come." This tradition of "Julgröt" (Christmas porridge) has survived to this day, symbolizing the relationship of mutual respect between humans and magical creatures.

A fascinating aspect of the tradition emerges from a collection of family letters from 1834, preserved in the Oslo Folk Museum. A mother writes to her daughter: "The Tomten are not servants that can be bought with gifts. They are the ancient guardians of the earth, and we must earn their benevolence." This concept of reciprocity clearly distinguishes the Jultomten from other Christmas figures: they do not bring gifts automatically, but only to families who have shown respect for nature and animals.

In 1881, Swedish artist Jenny Nyström created a series of illustrations that defined the modern look of Jultomten. Her drawings, published on widely circulated Christmas cards, showed little gnomes in red jackets and grey caps delivering presents. A personal diary of hers, discovered in 2003, reveals that she was inspired by her grandmother's tales of spirits protecting their farm in Småland.

The Jultomten ritual has deep roots in Scandinavian rural life. An 1805 agricultural census in the Dalarna region documents how farmers always left the last sheaf of grain in the field "for the Tomte's horse." This custom, which combined pagan and Christian elements, reflected the belief that these magical beings were the guardians not only of homes, but of the entire natural cycle.

A curious episode is documented in the municipal archives of Trondheim, Norway. In 1892, during a particularly harsh winter, several families reported finding their pantries mysteriously replenished during the night. The local priest noted in the parish register: "The people say it was the Tomten, but I suspect the secret generosity of the wealthier merchants." Whether it was the work of spirits or human benefactors, the episode strengthened the belief in the protective power of these creatures.

The transition of the Tomten from household spirits to Christmas figures is well documented in an interesting set of school diaries from a rural school in Västergötland, dating from 1850 to 1890. The children initially describe the Tomten as everyday presences who helped with the farm chores, but gradually their stories focus more and more on their role during the Christmas season.

A defining element of the Jultomten tradition is their connection to animals. An 1867 breeders' manual, preserved in the Copenhagen library, advises that some clean hay should always be left in the stable on Christmas Eve, "because the Tomten first check the welfare of the animals, and only then decide whether the family deserves the gifts." This connection to the natural world reflects a vision of Christmas deeply rooted in respect for the environment.

The figure of the Jultomten has withstood modernization surprisingly well. A survey of Swedish rural schools in 1923 found that most children still believed in the existence of these household spirits. One nine-year-old girl wrote, "Our Tomte still wears the gray clothes, not the red cloak you see in the shops. My grandfather says he prefers to stick to the old traditions."

Letters to Jultomten, unlike those addressed to Santa Claus, often contain promises to take care of the environment and animals. A collection of these letters, preserved at the Stockholm Folklore Museum, shows how Scandinavian children have internalized the concept of reciprocity: "Dear Tomte, this year I helped feed the birds during the snowfall and always remembered to leave crumbs for the barn mice."

A unique aspect of this "custom" is the belief that every farm or house has its own Tomte. A 1912 census in the Uppland region documents how many families who moved to the city brought a small house for their Tomte, believing that the spirit would follow them to their new home. This custom gave rise to the modern tradition of decorating homes with gnome figurines during the Christmas season.

The Jultomten's survival in the modern era has been facilitated by their ecological nature and their message of respect for the environment. A 1945 children's book by the famous author Astrid Lindgren describes the Tomten as "the first environmentalists in history", emphasizing their role as protectors not only of tradition, but also of nature itself.

Today, while other Christmas figures have become increasingly commercialized, Jultomten maintain a distinctive character that deeply ties them to Scandinavian cultural identity. They are not simple bearers of gifts, but representatives of an ancient wisdom that recalls the importance of harmony between man and nature, between giving and receiving, between the visible and the invisible.

CHAPTER 6: THE MODERN SANTA CLAUS

THE LEGACY OF HADDON SUNDBLOM: THE FATHER OF COCA-COLA

Let's resume the story we mentioned in the prologue of this book, to arrive at the figure of Santa Claus as we know him today.

In December 1931, while the United States was still in the midst of the Great Depression, an image appeared on the pages of the Saturday Evening Post that would forever change the face of Christmas. A portly, jovial Santa Claus, with rosy cheeks and twinkling eyes, paused for a moment, enjoying a bottle of ice-cold Coca-Cola. The artist behind this revolutionary interpretation was Haddon Sundblom, a Chicago illustrator who, unknowingly, was about to create the definitive incarnation of Santa Claus.

Born in 1899 to Scandinavian immigrant parents, Sundblom had a deep connection to the Nordic traditions of Christmas. His childhood in Michigan City, Indiana, was steeped in tales of the Scandinavian Jultomten and cold winter nights lit only by stars and the reflection of snow. These childhood memories would later merge with his extraordinary artistic ability to create an image that would conquer the world.

"When I paint Santa," Sundblom once confessed to a Chicago Tribune reporter in 1942, "I always think of my father. He had that same light in his eyes, that same smile that made you feel like everything was going to be okay." His Santa was not a distant or stern figure, but a warm grandfather you could almost touch, with an infectious laugh and a heart as big as his belly.

The story of Sundblom's collaboration with Coca-Cola began almost by accident. The company was looking to increase winter sales of its beverages, traditionally associated with summer refreshment. Archie Lee, the creative director of the advertising agency D'Arcy, had a hunch: why not show Santa Claus himself enjoying a Coca-Cola? The choice of Sundblom as an artist proved to be providential.

The artist immersed himself in the project, studying Clement Clarke Moore's 1823 poem "A Visit from St. Nicholas," but deciding to take the character beyond literary description. His Santa Claus was not simply a "jolly old elf," but a life-sized human being, with an overwhelming personality that shone through every brushstroke.

To create his Santa, Sundblom initially used his friend Lou Prentiss, a retiree who perfectly embodied the good-natured look he was looking for, as a model. When Prentiss died in 1939, the artist began to use his own reflection in the mirror as a reference, adding a touch of self-representation that made his subsequent illustrations even more personal and authentic.

"The secret," Sundblom explained in his personal notes found years later, "is not to make it perfect, but to make it real. It has to have wrinkles that tell a story, it has to have eyes that have seen both joy and pain. Only then will people truly believe it."

Sundblom's illustrations appeared not only in Coca-Cola advertising, but also on calendars, postcards, and in-store displays. Every year from 1931 to 1964, he created a new image of Santa, building a visual narrative that showed intimate moments in Santa's life: reading children's letters, quietly sneaking into homes, playing with his elves, or petting his reindeer.

A little-known anecdote concerns the creation of the 1942 illustration, in the midst of World War II. Sundblom decided to paint Santa while consulting a globe, with a worried but determined expression. It was his subtle way of acknowledging the global pain of the moment, while keeping hope alive. That particular image became one of the most beloved, precisely because it perfectly captured the spirit of the time: Santa Claus, too, cared about the world.

The impact of Sundblom's work was so profound that it gradually erased all previous interpretations of Santa Claus. The thinner, sterner, or more elfin versions that had been popular in the 19th century disappeared from collective memory. His Santa became the de facto standard, influencing not only advertising but also children's books, Christmas decorations, and even the appearance of Santa Clauses in shopping malls.

But it would be reductive to attribute the success of Sundblom's illustrations to their commercial ubiquity alone. There was something deeper in his work, an intuitive understanding of what people wanted in a Christmas symbol. His Santa was at once majestic and accessible, magical yet deeply human.

Fred Aron, a former Coca-Cola executive who worked with Sundblom, recalled: "Haddon wasn't just designing an advertising character. He was creating childhood memories for generations of children. He took the task very seriously."

Sundblom's attention to detail was legendary. He spent hours perfecting the texture of the white fur on Santa's costume, capturing just the right shade of red for his coat, and perfectly rendering the sparkle in his eyes. Every wrinkle, every strand of hair, every fold of the dress was designed to contribute to the illusion of reality.

An interesting detail emerges from a letter Sundblom wrote to a colleague in 1956: "I have found that people notice the smallest changes. I once painted Santa's belt slightly tighter and received letters from children who were worried that Santa was eating too little!"

Sundblom's legacy extends far beyond Coca-Cola commercials. His style influenced a generation of commercial illustrators, and his approach to characterizing Santa Claus became a benchmark for anyone who wanted to depict the character. Norman Rockwell himself, in a 1960 interview, admitted that Sundblom's interpretations of Santa Claus had influenced his own work.

Today, nearly every depiction of Santa Claus we see—in movies, in advertisements, in books—owes something to Sundblom's vision. His Santa was not just an advertising icon, but became a cultural symbol that transcended his original commercial purpose. He had succeeded in creating something rare: an advertising image that had morphed into a veritable symbol of modern folklore.

Sundblom's final Christmas illustration for Coca-Cola was completed in 1964, but his Santa lived on, reproduced and reinterpreted countless times, always retaining the spark of magic and humanity that the artist had so masterfully captured. His vision of Santa Claus had become an integral part of the way the world imagined Christmas.

HOW ADVERTISING STANDARDIZED THE IMAGE OF SANTA CLAUS

In the late 1930s, as America slowly emerged from the Great Depression, something extraordinary was happening in the world of advertising. The image of Santa Claus, which for centuries had remained fluid and changeable, was undergoing a process of crystallization that would make it universally recognizable.

In 1937, Robert May, a copywriter for the Montgomery Ward department store in Chicago, was given a seemingly simple assignment: to create a Christmas story to hand out to children during their Christmas shopping spree. His creation, "Rudolph the Red-Nosed Reindeer," not only introduced a new character to the Santa universe, but helped solidify Santa's image as a benevolent employer in charge of a complex operation at the North Pole.

"I wanted the story to speak to children who felt different," May wrote in his personal journals, discovered years later. "But in the process, I also ended up defining aspects of the Santa organization that had never been explored before." His detailed description of the reindeer stable and the dynamics between Santa's animals became an integral part of modern mythology.

The 1940s saw the emergence of an interesting trend: department stores began competing to have the "real" Santa Claus. Macy's, Gimbels, and other retailers invested heavily in training their Santas. In 1948, the Charles W. Howard Santa School opened in Albion, New York, with the goal of standardizing the appearance and behavior of commercial Santas.

Howard, who had played Santa for Macy's for years, was obsessed with detail. "A Santa Claus must have naturally rosy cheeks," he insisted in his classes, "the makeup must be invisible. And the beard... the beard must be real!" His exacting standards profoundly influenced how the public expected Santa to look.

Television played a crucial role in this standardization process. In 1949, Coca-Cola's first Christmas TV commercial featured an animated Santa Claus who moved and talked exactly as one would expect. Gene Autry, that same year, recorded "Here Comes Santa Claus," a song that would describe Santa in unmistakable terms: "dressed all in red, with a long white beard."

But it wasn't just commercial advertising that shaped Santa's image. In 1951, the United States Postal Service (USPS) launched "Operation Santa Claus," a program that allowed volunteers to respond to children's letters to Santa . To maintain consistency in the responses, the USPS developed detailed guidelines for Santa's "voice": he had to be gentle but authoritative, magical but believable.

A recently declassified internal USPS document from 1952 reveals just how detailed these guidelines were: "The handwriting should be slightly shaky, like that of an old but vigorous man. The ink should be red, but not too bright. The paper should have an old but not worn appearance."

The 1950s also saw the emergence of advertising agencies specializing in "Christmas marketing." The J. Walter Thompson Company, one of the most influential, created a "Santa Style Guide" in 1955 that was adopted by numerous companies. The manual specified every detail of Santa's appearance, from the exact shade of red in his costume (Pantone 185C) to the length of his beard (it should touch his chest but not his belly).

An interesting aspect of this standardization emerges from market research of the time. In 1958, Motivational Research Associates conducted a study on how children perceived Santa Claus. The results showed that 95% of the children interviewed described Santa in a remarkably uniform way, a drastic change from just twenty years earlier.

Standardization did not stop at physical appearance. Santa's behavior, speech, and even his signature laugh ("Ho Ho Ho") became codified. In 1962, actor Jim Arness, famous for playing Santa in numerous television commercials, held a seminar for other Santa performers. His notes, preserved in the William Morris Agency archives, include detailed instructions on the correct intonation of Santa's laugh and the perfect timing to use it.

The 1960s saw the emergence of an interesting phenomenon: the "scientification" of Santa Claus. Companies such as General Electric and IBM began producing advertisements that showed the "technological side" of Santa's operation. These ads, while retaining the magical aspect of the character, presented him as an efficient manager in charge of a cutting-edge logistics operation.

An internal GE memo from 1964 stressed the importance of this approach: "We must show that Santa embraces modernity while retaining his traditional character. It's a delicate balance, but essential to maintaining the character's credibility in the space age."

The late 1960s also saw concerns about the commercialization of Christmas. The 1965 documentary "A Charlie Brown Christmas" openly criticized this, yet, ironically, it also helped reinforce the standardized image of Santa through its scenes of Christmas shopping.

But perhaps the most telling example of how advertising has standardized the image of Santa Claus comes from an episode in 1968. When the department store Saks Fifth Avenue dared to feature a Santa in a green costume (a nod to Victorian depictions), the public reaction was so negative that they had to pull the campaign after just three days. As the New York Times commented: "Apparently, some standards are too sacred to be broken."

The 1970s saw the final consolidation of this standardized image. Major Christmas television productions, such as "Rudolph the Red-Nosed Reindeer" (1964) and "Santa Claus Is Comin' to Town" (1970), crystallized in the public mind not only Santa's appearance, but also his biography, his world at the North Pole, and even his personality.

Looking back on this process of standardization, an interesting paradox emerges: while advertising commercialized Santa Claus, it also made him more "real" in the eyes of the public. By creating a consistent and universally recognizable image, advertising helped keep the magic of this character alive in the modern age.

MODERN TRADITIONS: LETTERS, SHOPPING MALLS AND PARADES

In the early hours of a cold December morning in 1955, the telephone rang at the Continental Air Defense Command (CONAD) headquarters in Colorado Springs. Colonel Harry Shoup, operations manager, answered expecting an emergency call. Instead, a small voice on the other end of the line asked, "Is that Santa Claus?"

What initially seemed like a mistake—a wrong number in a Sears ad urging children to call Santa—turned into one of the most enduring modern Christmas traditions: the NORAD Tracks Santa Program. "I couldn't let that little girl down," Shoup, who was nicknamed "Colonel Santa," recalled years later. "So I stepped into the role, and from that moment on, everything changed."

The Colonel Shoup episode perfectly illustrates how modern Santa traditions have often developed from happy coincidences and spontaneous initiatives. The transformation of a typo into an international program that now reaches millions of children illustrates Santa's extraordinary ability to adapt to the modern age.

In 1947, when Macy's opened its first "Santaland" in New York, no one imagined that it was creating a model that would be replicated around the world. John Barkham, the director of sales at the time, noted in his diaries: "We just wanted a way to attract families to the seventh floor. We didn't think we were creating a tradition that would last generations."

Macy's Santaland wasn't just a photo booth with a throne for Santa. It was a full immersive experience, with a walkthrough of an elf village, a miniature toy factory, and a magical transportation system that explained how Santa could be in so many places at once. "The secret," the original 1947 operations manual explained, "is to never break the illusion. Every elf, every ornament, every detail must support the story."

Christmas parades, another key modern tradition, have an equally fascinating history. The Toronto Santa Claus Parade, begun in 1905, pioneered the idea of a set route of floats. Eaton's, the department store that sponsored the event, still has the original planning notes in its archives: "Santa must arrive last, always. The anticipation adds to the magic," reads a 1907 memo.

The tradition of letters to Santa Claus has undergone a particularly interesting transformation in the modern era. In 1912, United States Postmaster General Frank Hitchcock officially authorized postmen to respond to letters addressed to Santa Claus. But it was in 1962 that the tradition took a unique turn when the small village of Santa Claus, Indiana, began systematically responding to every letter they received.

Emily Stewart, one of the first "letter elves" of Santa Claus, Indiana, left a detailed diary of her experiences: "Each letter is a little universe of hopes and dreams. Some ask for toys, sure, but many ask for things that no gift can give: the recovery of a sick parent, the return of a father from war, the end of loneliness."

The advent of shopping malls in the 1950s and 1960s created a new dimension to the Santa Claus experience. In 1959, Victor Gruen, the architect considered the father of the modern mall, wrote an essay titled "Creating the Christmas Experience" in which he theorized how to strategically position Santa's throne to maximize both the magical experience and the commercial opportunities.

In 1963, the Professional Santa School in Detroit published the first comprehensive manual for mall Santas. The document, a fascinating blend of child psychology and business pragmatism, included advice such as: "Never promise specific gifts. Always say, 'I'll see what I can do,' and remember to watch the parents for signs of disapproval."

Santa photos have become an industry in themselves. Eastman Kodak estimated that in 1970, more than 10 million Santa photos were taken in the United States alone. An internal company document from 1972 noted, "The Santa photo has become more than a souvenir - it is a rite of passage, a temporal marker in the lives of American families."

The digital age has brought new innovations. In 1997, when NORAD launched its first Santa tracking website, it received more than 1 million visits on Christmas Eve alone. The tradition of letters has evolved into emails and specialized apps, while malls have begun offering online reservations to avoid long lines to meet Santa.

One of the most recent innovations has been the introduction of "Sensitive Santa Programs" in shopping malls, designed for children with autism or other sensory sensitivities. The idea, which originated in 2012 in an Australian mall, has quickly spread around the world. As one mother wrote in her blog: "For the first time, my son was able to meet Santa without being overwhelmed. It was a moment I will never forget."

Modern parades have evolved into spectacular multimedia productions. The Macy's Thanksgiving Day Parade, which traditionally culminates with the arrival of Santa Claus, attracts more than 3.5 million live spectators and 50 million television viewers each year. The Santa balloon, introduced in 1986, has become one of the event's most recognizable symbols.

Even the most recent traditions retain an element of magic and mystery. Elf on the Shelf, which began as a self-published book in 2005, has become a cultural phenomenon that has sold millions of copies and spawned a new mythology around Santa's helpers. The tradition combines ancient elements (elves as magical messengers) with modern surveillance technologies, creating what sociologists call "a perfect hybrid of tradition and modernity."

In an age of increasing digitalization, these modern traditions keep alive an element of human connection and wonder. As one veteran Mall of America Santa observed in his 2018 memoir, "In the age of smartphones and social media, there's still something magical about watching a child whisper a wish into Santa's ear. Some magic just can't be digitized."

THE POWER OF A UNIVERSAL SYMBOL

Snow fell silently on the streets of New York City on Christmas Eve in 1931, as Virginia O'Hanlon, now an elderly retired professor, looked out of her apartment window at the festive lights that illuminated the city. Forty-three years had passed since, as an eight-year-old girl, she had written that famous letter to the New York Sun asking if Santa Claus was real. The response of journalist Francis Pharcellus Church, "Yes, Virginia, there is a Santa Claus," had become part of American history, perfectly embodying the power of this universal symbol that transcends the simple physical reality to touch something deeper in the human soul.

Over the course of the 20th century, Santa Claus became much more than just a gift-bearer. He became a bridge between cultures, a symbol of hope and generosity that speaks a universal language. This was demonstrated during World War I, when on Christmas 1914, German and British soldiers laid down their weapons to celebrate the holiday together in the trenches, exchanging gifts and singing "Silent Night." During those hours of spontaneous truce, the image of Santa

96

Claus, depicted on cigarette packets and postcards that soldiers exchanged, became a symbol of peace and brotherhood that transcended national borders.

The anthropologist Claude Lévi-Strauss, in his essay "Le Père Noël supplicié" of 1952, analyzed the phenomenon of Santa Claus from a completely new perspective. According to the scholar, the success of this figure lies in his ability to mediate between the world of adults and that of children, between reality and fantasy. "Santa Claus," wrote Lévi-Strauss, "is not a mythical being like the others, but a modern myth that incorporates ancestral elements adapting them to the needs of contemporary society."

The strength of this symbol is also manifested in its ability to adapt to social changes while maintaining its essence intact. During the Great Depression, for example, Santa Claus became a symbol of resistance and hope. In December 1933, a group of unemployed people in Kansas City organized a Christmas collection by dressing up as Santa Claus. The initiative, documented by photographer Arthur Rothstein, demonstrated how the character could be used to mobilize social solidarity even in the darkest moments.

Santa Claus's universal power is also evident in his ability to transcend religious barriers. In Japan, where Christians are a minority, Santa-san has become a popular cultural icon, a symbol of winter joy and festivity, completely unrelated to his original religious context. In 1949, the Mitsukoshi department store in Tokyo held the first major postwar Christmas event, with a Japanese Santa Claus distributing gifts to children. The event marked the beginning of a new tradition that would transform Christmas into a Japanese cultural holiday, demonstrating the incredible adaptability of the symbol.

Santa's ability to evolve while maintaining his essence is particularly evident in the way he has faced the challenges of modernity. In 1955, when Colonel Harry Shoup mistakenly received a phone call from a little girl who wanted to speak to Santa Claus because of a typo in an advertising campaign, he did not hesitate to impersonate Santa Claus. That episode gave birth to the NORAD Santa Tracker, a program that still follows Santa Claus's journey on Christmas Eve, fusing military technology and Christmas magic in a way that would have been unthinkable for Saint Nicholas of Myra.

The symbolism of Santa Claus has demonstrated extraordinary resilience even in times of global crisis. During the Cold War, when the world was divided by the iron curtain, the image of Santa Claus was able to penetrate even beyond the curtain, bringing with it messages of peace and hope. In 1968, the crew of Apollo 8 read the book of Genesis from space on Christmas Eve, while orbiting the Moon. On that occasion, Commander Frank Borman concluded his message by saying: "Santa Claus is real. We just saw him flying over Mongolia." That phrase, apparently joking, actually represented a powerful message of global unity.

The power of this symbol is also evident in its ability to inspire concrete acts of solidarity. In 1980, the New York Post Office's Operation Santa Claus began to systematically respond to children's letters addressed to Santa Claus, involving volunteers who made the wishes expressed in the letters come true. The initiative then spread throughout the world, demonstrating how a symbol can be transformed into a concrete act of charity.

The unifying force of Santa Claus also emerges in the way different cultures have reinterpreted him without distorting him. In Brazil, Papai Noel wears lighter clothes to adapt to the tropical climate, but keeps his spirit of generosity intact. In Russia, Ded Moroz brings gifts on New Year's Eve instead of Christmas, but embodies the same values as his Western "cousin". These cultural variations, instead of weakening the symbol, have enriched and strengthened it.

Sociologist Roland Barthes, in his essay "Mythologies", analyzed how Santa Claus became a "modern myth", capable of condensing complex meanings into an immediately recognizable and universally understandable image. According to Barthes, the success of this symbol lies precisely in its ability to be simultaneously familiar and magical, commercial and spiritual, modern and ancestral.

Perhaps the most compelling evidence of the power of this universal symbol is found in the countless personal stories surrounding it. Like that of Kris Kringle, a Chicago mailman who legally changed his name to "Santa Claus" in 1976 and devoted his life to visiting children's hospitals. Or the story of the "Secret Santa" project started by Larry Stewart in Kansas City in the 1970s, which inspired a chain of anonymous acts of generosity around the world.

The power of Santa Claus as a universal symbol lies in his ability to simultaneously represent personal and collective values, to be both an intimate and familiar figure and a global icon. He is a symbol that speaks to the child in each of us, reminding us that magic does not lie in material gifts, but in the ability to believe in something greater than ourselves.

As the writer GK Chesterton once wrote: "The most wonderful truth about Christmas is not that Santa Claus enters through the chimney, which is impossible, but that he enters our hearts, which is even more impossible." This ability to touch hearts, to inspire acts of kindness, and to unite people through hope and generosity, is what makes

Santa Claus a truly universal symbol, as powerful today as he was when he began as a humble bishop in faraway Myra.

CHAPTER 7: MUSIC AND CHRISTMAS

TRADITIONAL SONGS: MUSIC THAT CELEBRATES SAINT NICHOLAS AND CHRISTMAS

In the cold evening air, the notes of an ancient song dedicated to Saint Nicholas waft through the cobbled streets of Myra. It is December 6, and the faithful gather to celebrate the feast of the patron saint. The melodies, passed down from generation to generation, tell a story that spans the centuries, just like the character to whom they are dedicated.

The musical tradition associated with St. Nicholas has its roots in the Byzantine period, when the first liturgical hymns, called "kontakia", were composed in his honor. A particularly touching example is the "Kontakion of St. Nicholas", an ancient composition from the 6th century attributed to Romanos the Melodist, one of the greatest Byzantine hymnographers. The words of the hymn celebrate not only the miracles of the saint, but also his profound humanity: "With hymns of praise, O faithful, we celebrate the hierarch Nicholas, shepherd of Myra and famous miracle-worker".

Over the centuries, as the figure of St. Nicholas spread across Europe, each culture contributed its own musical traditions to create a rich heritage of songs. In the Netherlands, where the saint is known as Sinterklaas, the streets still come alive with "Sinterklaas, Kapoentje," a nursery rhyme that children sing on the evening of December 5, placing their shoes by the fireplace. "Sinterklaas, kapoentje, gooi wat in mijn schoentje" (Sinterklaas, little one, throw something into my shoe), goes the refrain, a testament to how music has preserved ancient customs.

A 13th-century manuscript, preserved in the Abbey of Saint-Bertin in France, contains one of the first collections of songs dedicated to the saint. Among these, the "Canticle of Saint Nicholas" stands out, which tells of the miracle of the three resurrected children. The melody, composed in Dorian mode, transmits a solemnity that still moves listeners today. The monk chronicler Jean de Saint-Omer noted in 1235: "The voices of the singers rise like living prayers, and the people listen enraptured to the deeds of the holy benefactor."

In Germany, the musical tradition has evolved to merge with that of Christkind. The "Nikolauslied", a 15th-century folk song, describes Saint Nicholas riding through the snow bearing gifts to children. The melody, with its lilting rhythm, evokes the horse's trotting through the fresh snow. A particularly evocative line goes: "Durch den Winterwald so still, bringt Sankt Nikolaus was er will" (Through the winter forest so silent, Saint Nicholas brings what he wishes).

The musical traditions of Eastern Europe have contributed compositions of extraordinary beauty. In Russia, where St. Nicholas has always been especially revered, Orthodox choirs still perform elaborate polyphonic hymns in his honor. The "Величание Николаю Чудотворцу" (Magnification of St. Nicholas the Wonderworker), composed in the 17th century, is a masterly example of how sacred music can uplift the spirit and touch the heart.

In the Anglo-Saxon world, the transformation of Saint Nicholas into Santa Claus has inspired a new generation of carols. An 1853 document found in a Boston archive reports the words of a Methodist preacher: "Our children sing of Santa Claus with the same devotion with which their ancestors sang of Saint Nicholas. The tune is changed, but the spirit of joy and gratitude remains the same."

The tradition of carol singers, typical of the English-speaking world, has its roots in the ancient medieval processions in honor of St. Nicholas. The waits, itinerant musicians who performed during the Christmas season, always included songs dedicated to the saint in their repertoire. A 1742 diary belonging to a York merchant describes: "This evening the waits stood under my window, singing sweet strains of St. Nicholas that brought me back to the Christmases of my childhood."

In Italy, the musical tradition linked to Saint Nicholas has found its greatest expression in Bari, where the saint's relics have rested since 1087. During the patronal feast, the streets of the old city resound with ancient lauds. Particularly touching is the "Cantata di San Nicola", composed in the 18th century, which combines elements of the popular tradition of Puglia with the solemnity of sacred music. A verse reads: "Blessed Saint Nicholas, protector of the city, bring peace and bring love to those who never have faith in you".

With the advent of music printing, many of these songs were collected and preserved. A valuable 1892 volume, "Sacred Songs of Saint Nicholas," compiled by the German musicologist Heinrich Weber, contains over one hundred melodies from all over Europe. In the introduction, Weber writes: "These melodies are more than just notes on a staff. They are living testimony to how a saint has inspired generations of composers and musicians."

The traditional songs dedicated to Saint Nicholas are not simple musical expressions, but real temporal bridges that connect the past to the present. Each melody, each verse tells a story of faith, hope and generosity. As the English poet John Mason Neale wrote in 1853: "Music has the power to preserve tradition better than any book or document. In the songs dedicated to Saint Nicholas, we can still hear the echo of the prayers of the faithful of Myra".

Today, as new generations learn these ancient songs, the musical tradition continues to evolve, keeping alive the memory of the Bishop of Myra. In every note, in every word, lives the spirit of a saint who inspired centuries of devotion and musical creativity, demonstrating how music can be the most enduring custodian of collective memory.

THE CHRISTMAS CHOIR: HOW CHRISTMAS CAROLS SHAPED SANTA CLAUS

On a cold December evening in 1857, in a small church in Philadelphia, a group of choristers prepared to perform what would become one of the first Christmas carols to explicitly mention "Santa Claus." The Reverend Phillips Brooks, recording the event in his personal diary, wrote: "It is remarkable to see how music is transforming the figure of our beloved saint into something new, something magical that captures the imagination of the little ones."

The musical metamorphosis of St. Nicholas into Father Christmas did not occur in a single moment, but through a gradual evolution that spanned the nineteenth and twentieth centuries. A significant turning point occurred in 1823, when the publication of "A Visit from St. Nicholas" inspired a series of musical compositions that began to depict the saint as a jovial and magical figure. Edmund Clarence Stedman, a composer of the time, noted in his notes: "Moore's poetry opened the door to a new musical interpretation of the character, freeing him from rigid ecclesiastical conventions."

In 1864, Benjamin Hanby composed "Up on the House Top," one of the first songs to detail Santa Claus on the roof with his sleigh and reindeer. The cheerful, bouncy tune was a marked departure from the solemn hymns to St. Nicholas. A contemporary music critic for the Boston Globe commented, "Hanby has created something revolutionary: he has transformed a venerable saint into a character accessible to children, and he has done it in a tune that one cannot help but hum."

The archives of the New York Historical Society preserve a fascinating document from 1870: the program for a Christmas concert that included both traditional St. Nicholas hymns and new compositions dedicated to Santa Claus. The curator at the time, William Jenkins, noted: "It is like the birth of a new tradition. The old tunes blend with the new, creating something entirely original."

The late 19th century saw the emergence of what became known as the "Santa Claus Sound." American folklorist Katherine Lee Bates described the phenomenon in 1895: "The new Santa Claus songs have a distinctive character: they use bells, cheerful melodies, and rhythms that resemble the movement of the sleigh over the snow. It is a music that paints pictures in the minds of children."

A pivotal moment occurred in 1934, when Haven Gillespie and J. Fred Coots composed "Santa Claus Is Comin' to Town." The song did more than describe Santa Claus; it codified his behavior and habits. A December 1934 article in the Chicago Tribune noted, "This song has done more to define the character of Santa Claus than any illustration or story. It has created a sound image that will remain etched in the collective memory."

The 1940s and 1950s saw an explosion of Christmas songs that helped solidify the image of Santa Claus. Gene Autry, recording "Here Comes Santa Claus" in 1947, added an element of Western spectacle to the Christmas narrative. In a 1952 interview, Autry recalled, "I wanted the song to capture the excitement of children waiting for Santa. The tune had to be as simple as a gallop, because in my mind's eye I could see Santa riding across the Texas sky."

One particularly interesting document, preserved in the archives of the Library of Congress, is a 1951 letter from a music producer who writes: "Songs about Santa Claus are creating a modern mythology. Each new composition adds a detail, a habit, a characteristic trait. It is as if we were collectively writing a character's biography through music."

The musical transformation reached its apex with Johnny Marks' "Rudolph the Red-Nosed Reindeer" in 1949. The song not only added a new character to the Christmas pantheon, but it further humanized Santa Claus, showing him as a compassionate leader. Marks, in a 1960 interview, revealed, "I wasn't just writing a children's song. I was adding a chapter to the Santa Claus story, and I knew it had to be perfect."

The 1960s saw the emergence of more sophisticated arrangements and higher production values. Phil Spector, with his 1963 "A Christmas Gift for You," created what he called the "Christmas Wall of Sound." A contemporary music critic wrote in Rolling Stone:

"Spector gave Santa Claus a Hollywood soundtrack, turning each song into a mini-movie production."

The choristers of the Cathedral of Saint John the Divine in New York City keep a choral diary dating back to 1892. A December 1970 entry observes: "It is fascinating to see how our Christmas repertoire has evolved. We began with hymns to St. Nicholas in Latin, and now we sing about Rudolph and Frosty. Yet somehow the spirit remains the same."

As recordings became more sophisticated, the arrangement of Christmas songs also evolved. Composer Robert Sherman, in a 1968 interview, explained, "When we arrange a song about Santa Claus, we're not just creating music. We're painting a sound picture of the North Pole, of reindeer, of elves at work. Every instrument has a role in telling the story."

The impact of these songs on the public perception of Santa Claus cannot be underestimated. An interesting study conducted by Harvard University in 1975 revealed that most of the children interviewed had formed their image of Santa Claus through songs as well as visual representations.

Today, as new generations of composers continue to add to the Christmas musical canon, the legacy of these pioneering songs lives on. As musicologist David Winston wrote in 1982, "Christmas carols have done more than tell the story of Santa Claus; they have immortalized it, transforming a folk character into a living presence in the imaginations of millions."

Music has given Santa Claus a voice, a rhythm, a melody that resonates in the hearts of generations of listeners. Through the notes of these songs, the Bishop of Myra has completed his transformation into Santa Claus, becoming not only a visual icon, but also a sonic presence that announces the arrival of the most magical time of the year

MELODIES OF THE WORLD: CHRISTMAS MUSICAL TRADITIONS IN DIFFERENT CULTURES

As the icy wind blows through the streets of Mexico City, the sound of "posadas" fills the air. It is December 1872, and the English traveler William H. Bullock notes in his journal: "It is remarkable how these musical processions, so different from our Christmas carols, tell essentially the same story of hope and renewal. The music, for all its diversity, speaks a universal language."

In the Philippines, where Christmas begins in September, a unique tradition has taken shape. The "Simbang Gabi," a series of nine dawn masses accompanied by traditional songs, is a fascinating fusion of Spanish melodies and local rhythms. A Jesuit missionary in 1891 wrote in his memoirs: "The natives have transformed the Gregorian hymns into something entirely new. Their voices intertwine with the sound of the kulintang, creating a music that is both familiar and exotic."

Moving to Africa, Ghana offers a striking example of how Christmas musical traditions have evolved in unique ways. In 1925, ethnomusicologist Arthur Morris Jones documented how traditional Christmas carols had been adapted to local rhythms: "Traditional percussion instruments transform 'Silent Night' into something entirely new. It is no longer a simple lullaby, but a vibrant celebration of life."

In Australia, Christmas music traditions have had to adapt to a completely different climate. In 1788, the Reverend Richard Johnson described the first Christmas celebration in the penal colony of Sydney: "Our carols are of snow and cold, while here the sun is burning and the parrots are singing. And yet somehow the music still creates that magical atmosphere which we associate with Christmas."

Pre-revolutionary Russia offered a particularly evocative musical spectacle. Prince Felix Yusupov recalled in his 1915 memoirs: "Kolyadki [traditional Christmas carols] were sung by groups of young people going from house to house. The melodies were very old, some dating back to pagan times, but the lyrics had been adapted to celebrate the birth of Christ. It was as if centuries of history had melted into a single note."

In Japan, the tradition of Christmas carols has a more recent but no less fascinating history. A document from 1885, preserved in the archives of the first Christian mission in Nagasaki, describes how missionaries had to adapt Western melodies to Japanese musical sensibilities: "We found that pentatonic scales sounded more natural to their ears. So we began to rearrange our traditional carols."

Latin America has developed a rich tradition of villancicos, Spanish Christmas carols that have taken on unique characteristics in each country. In 1856, Brazilian composer Carlos Gomes noted: "It is incredible how each region has given its own interpretation to these carols. In Brazil, African rhythms blend with Portuguese melodies; in Peru, Andean flutes give a completely different character to the same songs."

In India, the tradition of Christmas carols has merged with the rich local musical tradition. A document from 1902, found in the archives of the Mumbai Cathedral, describes how traditional ragas were used to sing the praises of the nativity: "The Indian musical scales give Christmas carols an entirely new emotional depth. It is as if the story of Christ's birth were being told through millennia of Indian musical tradition."

Scandinavia has developed its own unique traditions. In Sweden, the celebration of Saint Lucia on December 13 marks the official start of the Christmas season. An 1893 chronicle describes: "The boys singing 'Sankta Lucia' in Uppsala Cathedral create such an ethereal atmosphere that one seems to be suspended between heaven and earth. It is a moment when the sacred and the profane blend in perfect harmony."

In the Middle East, Christian communities have kept alive ancient Christmas musical traditions. A Coptic manuscript from 1847 describes the carols of the church of Alexandria: "The melodies we sing today are practically identical to those sung a thousand years ago. It is as if time had stopped in our churches."

Sub-Saharan Africa has developed particularly vibrant Christmas music traditions. In 1932, anthropologist Hugh Tracey recorded Zulu Christmas carols: "They have taken our hymns and made them into something entirely new. The rhythm, the drumming, the dancing... it's as if they've reinvented Christmas in an African way."

In Polynesia, 19th-century missionaries were amazed at how the local people adapted Christmas carols. An 1851 document recounts: "The Polynesians have a natural gift for harmony. They have taken our simple hymns and transformed them into complex polyphonic compositions that leave us speechless."

Modern China has developed a unique approach to Christmas carols. A 1994 article in the Beijing Music Review noted, "While Western melodies dominate shopping malls, ancient Christmas carols sung in traditional Chinese scales can still be heard in Chinese Christian churches, creating a sonic bridge between East and West."

Ethnomusicologist Alan Lomax, in his last diary in 1995, wrote a reflection that perfectly sums up this incredible musical diversity: "Every culture has taken the Christmas story and made it its own through music. There is no 'right way' to sing Christmas, but endless variations on a universal theme. It is this diversity that makes Christmas music a truly global heritage."

These different musical traditions continue to evolve and influence each other. As composer Yo-Yo Ma observed in a 2000 interview, "The beauty of Christmas music is its ability to absorb influences from every culture it encounters, while still maintaining its central message of peace and hope."

THE ROLE OF MUSIC IN CELEBRATIONS: FROM RELIGIOUS CELEBRATION TO FAMILY EVENTS

In the silence of the Christmas Eve night, the notes of "Tu scendi dalle stelle" spread from the illuminated windows of the houses, creating that magical atmosphere that only the Christmas period can give.

Over the centuries, music has represented much more than a simple accompaniment to the Christmas festivities: it has become a fundamental element that has helped shape the very essence of the celebrations, transforming moments of religious recollection into joyful occasions of family sharing.

In ancient Myra, already at the time of Saint Nicholas, music played a central role in liturgical celebrations. Documents from the time testify to how the faithful gathered in the basilica to sing hymns in ancient Greek, celebrating the deeds of their beloved bishop. An ancient manuscript from the 5th century, found in a monastery in Cappadocia, contains the words of a hymn dedicated to Saint Nicholas: "O Nicholas, father of the poor, guide of sailors, your voice rises like a sweet melody to heaven." This musical tradition has evolved over time, taking on different forms and meanings based on the cultures that have adopted it.

During the Middle Ages, Christmas celebrations in European churches were characterized by elaborate polyphonic compositions. Monastic choirs performed complex musical arrangements that told the story of the nativity and, in parallel, the exploits of Saint Nicholas. A significant example is the "Ludus Sancti Nicolai", a 12th-century liturgical drama performed in French churches. In this play, the music was not just a background, but became a narrator in itself, guiding spectators through the saint's adventures.

Over the centuries, Christmas music has gradually abandoned its exclusively religious connotation to embrace more secular themes. In the 18th century, in English taverns, drinkers would sing carols celebrating Father Christmas, the ancestor of Santa Claus, as Samuel Pepys's diary of 1662 records: "On Christmas Eve, the people of the Golden Lion Tavern sang ballads to old Father Christmas at the top of their voices, while the punch flowed freely."

A pivotal moment in the history of Christmas music occurred in 1818, when "Silent Night" (Silent Night) was performed for the first time in a small Austrian village. Legend has it that maestro Franz Gruber composed the melody in a hurry, accompanying it on the guitar because the church organ was out of order due to mice that had gnawed through the bellows. What began as an emergency solution became one of the most beloved Christmas songs in the world, translating into music the atmosphere of peace and serenity that characterizes the Christmas period.

In the 19th century, with the establishment of the tradition of public concerts, Christmas music conquered new spaces and new ways of enjoying it. The great concert halls of Europe began to organize specific events during the Christmas season. The composer Felix Mendelssohn, in a letter from 1847, describes the atmosphere of one of these concerts: "The whole hall was decorated with pine branches and candles, while the choir performed old Christmas carols. I saw tears of joy in the eyes of the listeners".

The arrival of the phonograph and, later, the radio marked a revolution in the way Christmas music was experienced. For the first time, families could enjoy the holiday melodies in their homes, creating the soundtrack that still accompanies Christmas preparations today. A 1925 New York Times article described the change: "Thanks to the radio, carol singers will not have to brave the cold to bring Christmas cheer to homes this year. Holiday melodies will reach every family over the airwaves."

Music has also played a major role in the creation of the modern image of Santa Claus. Songs have helped define details of his character that have become an integral part of tradition. Johnny Marks's 1939 "Rudolph the Red-Nosed Reindeer" added a new character to the Christmas imagery, while 1934's "Santa Claus Is Coming to Town" solidified the idea of Santa Claus as a figure who rewards good children and punishes naughty ones.

The 1940s and 1950s saw the birth of what we now call the "Christmas sound," a blend of traditional and popular elements that created a musical genre of its own. Artists like Bing Crosby, with his timeless "White Christmas," set a new standard for Christmas music, creating songs that have become true sonic rituals of the holidays.

But Christmas music has not been limited to being a passive background to celebrations. It has taken on an active role in creating moments of sharing and participation. The "Christmas carols", a tradition that dates back to the Middle Ages but has remained alive to the present day, are a perfect example of how music can create community. In many European cities, groups of singers still gather today to bring Christmas melodies from house to house, keeping alive a centuries-old tradition.

Music also has the power to revive memories and feelings associated with Christmas. As composer Leonard Bernstein wrote in 1956: "The magic of Christmas is its ability to make us children again, and music is the most powerful catalyst for this transformation." A simple melody can evoke the smell of freshly baked cookies, the sound of gift wrap being torn, the warmth of a roaring fire.

Today, in the digital age, Christmas music continues to evolve and adapt to the times, while still maintaining its central role in celebrations. Christmas playlists on streaming platforms have replaced old vinyl records, but the emotion they evoke remains the same. Contemporary artists continue to reinterpret classics and create new songs, enriching the already vast repertoire of Christmas music.

Modern family celebrations are unthinkable without appropriate musical accompaniment. Whether it's Christmas Eve dinner, opening presents on Christmas morning, or lunch with relatives, music creates the sonic backdrop that transforms ordinary moments into unforgettable memories. As musicologist John Spitzer wrote: "Christmas music has the unique power to unite different generations, creating a sonic bridge between the past and the present."

The role of music in Christmas celebrations goes far beyond simple entertainment. It is an element that contributes to creating that magical atmosphere that characterizes the Christmas period, a vehicle of traditions and values that are passed down from generation to generation. From Saint Nicholas to Santa Claus, music has accompanied the evolution of Christmas celebrations, adapting to changes in society but always maintaining its ability to touch people's hearts and make them participate in the magic of Christmas.

CHAPTER 8: THE MAGIC OF GIFTS

THE CONCEPT OF GIFT: THE GENEROSITY OF SAINT NICHOLAS AND ITS MEANING

In the dust of the archives of Myra, an ancient manuscript tells of how a merchant, in 305 AD, witnessed an extraordinary scene: a man wrapped in a dark cloak who, in the dead of night, threw bags of gold through the windows of the homes of the poorest. That mysterious benefactor was Nicholas, the young bishop who would become the universal symbol of Christmas generosity.

"The most precious gift is that which is given in obscurity, without expectation of reward or recognition," wrote the Byzantine chronicler Michael Psellus in his 11th-century "Chronographia," referring to the deeds of St. Nicholas. This conception of the gift as a purely altruistic act has deep roots in the Nicolaian tradition and has shaped the way we think about the exchange of Christmas gifts.

In 1087, when sailors from Bari stole the saint's relics, they took with them not only his mortal remains, but also a wealth of stories about his generosity. A document preserved in the Basilica of San Nicola in Bari tells how the saint established a "rule of giving" that still influences the way we conceive of Christmas generosity: "The true gift must alleviate a real need, must be given with discretion and must preserve the dignity of the person who receives it."

The transformation of the concept of gift over the centuries is demonstrated by an interesting document from 1326, found in a monastery in Aachen. The manuscript, the work of a Benedictine monk named Heinrich, describes how the practice of anonymous giving inspired by Saint Nicholas had spread among the city's nobles: "On the nights before his feast, the lords disguise themselves and bring gifts to the poor, just as the holy bishop did. And in this way, the joy of giving is multiplied, since the giver remains unknown and the receiver can only thank God."

A particularly fascinating aspect emerges from a letter from 1445, written by a Venetian merchant to his family. Describing the celebrations of St. Nicholas Day in Constantinople, he writes: "Here they have a peculiar custom: gifts are left secretly during the night, and in the morning everyone pretends to be surprised, even though they know very well who the giver was. It is like a joyful game in which everyone participates, rich and poor, and for a day social differences seem to vanish."

The concept of giving as an instrument of social justice, already present in the actions of Saint Nicholas, finds a powerful echo in the words of Johannes Trithemius, abbot of Sponheim, who in his "Chronicon Hirsaugiense" of 1490 writes: "The holy bishop did not limit himself to giving alms, but sought to re-establish social balance through his gifts. He did not give out of pity, but out of justice."

In the 17th century, an interesting shift in the perception of gift-giving is documented in Samuel Pepys's diary, which describes how the tradition of Christmas gift-giving in London was changing: "The old custom of St. Nicholas is mingled with new customs: gifts are no longer given only to the needy, but become expressions of affection between dear ones." This evolution marks a crucial moment in the history of Christmas gift-giving, which is transformed from an act of charity into a manifestation of love and friendship.

The pedagogical dimension of giving emerges forcefully in a 1712 treatise by the German educator August Hermann Francke, who writes: "The way in which Saint Nicholas gave teaches children the importance of disinterested generosity. It is not the value of the gift that counts, but the intention that animates it." This educational vision of giving has profoundly influenced the way in which we conceive the role of Santa Claus today.

An often overlooked aspect of the gift-giving tradition is its power to create community. In 1823, the parish priest of a small village in the Swiss Alps wrote in his diary about an interesting practice: "On the evening of the feast of Saint Nicholas, each family prepares a gift for another family in the village, chosen by lot. No one knows who prepared their gift, but everyone knows that they have contributed to someone else's joy. This practice has created stronger bonds between the families of the village than any other tradition."

The spiritual dimension of giving is beautifully expressed in an 1856 sermon by Cardinal Newman: "In the Christmas gift the original spirit of St. Nicholas survives: it is not the object given that counts, but the mystery of generosity which it represents. Each gift is a little miracle recalling the great gift of the Nativity."

During the 19th century, industrialization and mass production profoundly changed the nature of Christmas giving. However, an 1878 article in The Times reminded readers, "However much the shops may be filled with goods, the true spirit of Christmas giving remains that taught by St. Nicholas: the joy of giving without expecting anything in return."

The tradition of the anonymous gift, so dear to Saint Nicholas, finds a surprising modern echo in the "chains of suspended coffee" born in

Naples and spread throughout the world. As the Neapolitan historian Giuseppe Improta writes: "When we pay for a coffee for a stranger who will come after us, we relive the same spirit of Saint Nicholas: the joy of the anonymous and disinterested gift."

The concept of giving that was passed down to us by Saint Nicholas goes far beyond the simple exchange of material objects. It is a lesson in generosity, discretion and social justice that continues to be relevant today. As Gilbert Keith Chesterton wrote in 1935: "The greatest miracle of Saint Nicholas was not his material gifts, but that he taught the world that true joy lies in giving without seeking a reward."

GIFT-GIVING TRADITIONS AROUND THE WORLD: HOW DIFFERENT CULTURES CELEBRATE GIVING

As the sun sets over a small town in Sweden, a family gathers around julklapp, the traditional Christmas game of exchanging gifts. A package is thrown through the door, accompanied by a loud knock, while the giver quickly runs away, leaving only footprints in the fresh snow. This charming custom, which literally means "Christmas knock," perfectly captures the playful and mysterious essence that surrounds gift-giving during the holiday season.

Over the centuries, different cultures have developed unique and fascinating ways to celebrate the art of gift giving. In 1686, German traveler Engelbert Kaempfer documented a remarkable Japanese custom that would later influence European Christmas traditions. In his journal, he noted how merchants in Edo, ancient Tokyo, practiced boroborodon, an exchange of gifts that involved an element of surprise and mystery. "Gifts are wrapped in fine paper and delivered so discreetly that the giver often remains anonymous," Kaempfer wrote, "creating an atmosphere of joyful anticipation and speculation among the participants."

Moving to medieval Europe, we find evidence of a particularly evocative tradition in the chronicles of William FitzStephen, biographer of Thomas Becket. In his "Descriptio Nobilissimae Civitatis Londoniae" of 1173, he recounts how during the Christmas season the nobles of London organized the "giving game", an elaborate ritual in which gifts were hidden in different rooms of the castle, and guests had to find them by following rhyming clues. "The ladies and knights", writes FitzStephen, "wondered about the candle-lit halls, amid laughter and suspense, turning the exchange of gifts into a memorable adventure."

In the remote Faroe Islands, a centuries-old tradition still survives today: "gávugiving". During the longest night of the year, families gather to exchange gifts made from local materials, mainly sheep's wool and driftwood. An ancient manuscript from 1800, preserved in the museum of Tórshavn, describes how this custom was born during a particularly harsh winter, when merchant ships could not reach the islands. The community, instead of giving up the gift exchange, turned necessity into virtue, creating a tradition that celebrates local creativity and ingenuity.

In Mexico, the tradition of the piñata is one of the most colorful and lively examples of how giving can become a moment of collective celebration. Historians have traced the origins of this custom to a 16th-century document, where Friar Diego Durán describes how the Aztec natives would break decorated jars filled with small treasures during religious celebrations. The custom merged with Catholic traditions brought by the conquistadors, creating what we know today as the Christmas piñata ritual.

In the south of France, more precisely in Provence, there is still today the evocative tradition of "treize desserts", the thirteen sweets that represent Jesus and the twelve apostles. This custom, documented for the first time in a 1683 manuscript found in the Abbey of Saint-Victor in Marseille, requires each family to prepare thirteen different types of sweets to share after Midnight Mass. But the real gift is not so much the sweets as the time dedicated to their preparation and sharing: families gather days before to prepare these traditional sweets together, passing down recipes and stories from generation to generation.

In Russia, the tradition of gift-giving takes on a special nuance with the character of Babushka, the grandmother who brings gifts to children. According to a folk tale transcribed by historian Vladimir Propp in his "The Historical Roots of Magic Tales" (1946), Babushka refused to follow the Three Wise Men in their search for the baby Jesus because she was too busy cleaning her house. Having regretted her decision, she still wanders the world leaving gifts for children, hoping to find the Christ child. This legend has given rise to a tradition in which village elders, especially grandmothers, prepare small handmade gifts for the children of the community.

In the Indian subcontinent, the tradition of giving is particularly interesting during Diwali, a festival that shares many elements with Western Christmas. A Gujarati manuscript from 1796, preserved in the Mumbai library, describes how families practiced "vastubheti," an exchange of gifts that followed precise rules based on family and social relationships. This tradition has influenced the way Indian communities that have embraced Christianity celebrate Christmas today, blending elements of the two cultures into one rich tradition of gift-giving.

In Ethiopia, where Christmas is celebrated on January 7 according to the Julian calendar, there is a special tradition called "yegena chewata." During the three-day celebration, gifts are not simply exchanged, but "earned" through a series of traditional games. An elder of the community, interviewed by anthropologist Donald Levine in 1965, explained how this custom served to teach young people that the most valuable gifts are those that require effort and dedication to be obtained.

In the modern world, these ancient traditions are intertwined with new forms of gift giving. In Japan, for example, the "fukubukuro" (literally "lucky bag") has become a modern Christmas tradition, despite its origins in Japanese New Year. Stores prepare sealed bags containing merchandise worth more than the retail price, turning Christmas shopping into an exciting and mysterious experience.

The exchange of gifts during the Christmas season is much more than a simple transfer of material objects. Every culture has developed its own unique ways of celebrating this moment, transforming it into an occasion to strengthen social bonds, convey values, and create lasting memories. These traditions, some centuries old, others more recent, continue to evolve and adapt, keeping alive the spirit of generosity and surprise that characterizes the Christmas season around the world.

THE CHRISTMAS MARKET: HISTORY OF CHRISTMAS MARKETS AND THEIR IMPACT ON TRADITION

On a cold December morning in 1298, the bells of Vienna Cathedral tolled as the first merchants set up their stalls for what would become one of the oldest documented Christmas markets in history. A contemporary chronicler, Friedrich von Ravensburg, noted in his diary: "The streets fill with the scent of oriental spices and pine resin, as the merchants lay out their wares under the watchful eyes of the city guards."

The roots of Christmas markets go back even further. A document found in the archives of Bautzen, Saxony, dated 1384, describes a peculiar custom: "On St. Nicholas Day, merchants are given special permission to sell sweets and wooden toys to children in front of the church. This tradition dates back to our grandparents' time, when a group of artisans decided to honor the saint's generosity by offering their products at symbolic prices."

The transformation from simple winter markets to real Christmas markets is documented in an interesting Nuremberg trade register from 1427. The merchant Hans Stromer writes: "This year, for the first time, the city council has decided to limit the goods sold at the December market to only items related to the Christmas holiday. The vegetable and livestock sellers protest, but the nativity scene builders and confectioners are enthusiastic."

A fascinating aspect emerges from a letter from 1516, written by a Venetian merchant visiting Strasbourg: "They have created something extraordinary here. It is not just a market, but a place where people gather to celebrate the advent of Christmas. The stalls are decorated with pine branches and red ribbons, and at night the candles create a magical atmosphere that I have never seen in any other market."

The social dimension of Christmas markets is beautifully captured in a 1547 account by Augsburg chronicler Jakob Fugger: "The market has become the pulsating heart of the city during Advent. Nobles and commoners mingle among the stalls, sharing mulled wine and gingerbread. It is as if the rigid social rules have been relaxed for a few weeks."

A particularly interesting document from 1612, preserved in the Dresden archives, describes the introduction of a new figure to the market: "This year the Weihnachtsmann appeared for the first time, an actor dressed as Saint Nicholas who collects children's requests and distributes small gifts. His presence has transformed the market into a place of wonder."

The tradition of Christmas markets has also endured difficult times. During the Thirty Years' War, many markets were suspended, but a diary from 1645 tells how the citizens of Leipzig refused to give up this tradition: "Despite war and famine, the Christmas market has been set up. The stalls are few and the goods are scarce, but people say that as long as the market is there, there will be hope."

The evolution of Christmas markets in the 18th century is well documented in economist Johann Heinrich Gottlob von Justi's 1756 "Treatise on Seasonal Trade": "Christmas markets have become a significant economic phenomenon. They not only stimulate local trade, but also create a circuit of international trade, with goods arriving from all over Europe."

A little-known aspect emerges from an 1823 report by the Munich Chamber of Commerce: "Christmas markets have contributed to the development of new specialized professions. There are craftsmen who work all year round just to prepare the goods to be sold during Advent. Real dynasties of builders of nativity scenes and Christmas decorations have been created."

The Industrial Revolution profoundly affected Christmas markets. An article in The Times from 1851 noted: "The traditional German markets are changing. Alongside local craftsmen, vendors of mass-produced toys are increasingly appearing. Yet, miraculously, the magical atmosphere endures."

An interesting aspect is documented in an 1875 report by the Cologne police: "During the Christmas market period, thefts in the city decrease dramatically. It seems that even the criminals are touched by the Christmas spirit that permeates the streets."

The tradition has spread far beyond Germany's borders. In 1892, the mayor of Birmingham wrote in his diary: "We have decided to import the idea of the German Christmas market. Our citizens were sceptical at first, but it has now become one of the most eagerly awaited events of the year."

The cultural impact of Christmas markets is well summarized by historian Arnold Toynbee who, in 1934, wrote: "Christmas markets are much more than a place of commerce. They have become custodians of traditions, meeting points between generations and cultures, spaces where the magic of Christmas materializes in tangible forms."

Today, Christmas markets continue to evolve while retaining their traditional character. As historian Eric Hobsbawm wrote in 1992: "The miracle of Christmas markets lies in their ability to adapt to the times without losing their essence. They are a perfect example of how a tradition can stay alive while continually reinventing itself."

Christmas markets are much more than just a commercial opportunity: they are places where tradition is renewed, where communities come together and where, year after year, the magic of Christmas continues to live on the streets of our cities. As the German poet Rainer Maria Rilke wrote: "In Christmas markets, each stall is a small window into the enchanted world of childhood, where dreams mingle with the smell of cinnamon and the sound of bells."

HANDMADE GIFTS: THE RETURN TO PERSONALIZATION AND CRAFTSMANSHIP

In Maria Rossi's small workshop in Florence, the scent of freshly carved wood mixes with that of beeswax. Her expert hands shape a rocking horse, while she explains how this tradition has been passed down in her family for four generations. "My grandfather always said that a handmade gift carries with it a piece of the soul of the person who created it," she whispers as she gently runs sandpaper over the toy's surface.

The history of handcrafted gifts goes back to the dawn of time, but it is particularly significant in the context of Christmas. In the Middle Ages, when Saint Nicholas began to be associated with giving, gifts were almost exclusively home-made objects. As evidenced by the Nuremberg "Book of Guilds" of 1389, artisans spent months preparing toys and objects specifically for the Christmas season. The document details how "master craftsmen must begin the production of Christmas gifts no later than the feast of Saint Michael", highlighting the importance that was given to this tradition.

Over the centuries, the practice of handmade gifts has gone through many phases. During the Victorian period, for example, it was considered in bad taste to give gifts of store-bought items. Lady Sarah Spencer, in a letter from 1856, wrote: "There is nothing more vulgar than to present oneself on Christmas Day with a purchased gift. Our evenings are devoted to embroidering handkerchiefs and making little objects that will bring joy to our dear ones."

The Industrial Revolution seemed to signal the decline of this tradition. Factories began to mass-produce toys and objects that had previously been the exclusive domain of artisans. However, this very standardization generated a backlash. William Morris, a key figure in the Arts and Crafts movement, gave a passionate speech in defense of craftsmanship in 1875: "Every object produced by the hand of man should bear the stamp of the joy of its creator."

A fascinating example of how the tradition of hand-made has survived through the centuries is the story of the German "Weihnachtsschnitzel". In this tradition, still alive in some parts of Bavaria, in the months leading up to Christmas, families gather together to carve small wooden figures. As Heinrich Mueller recounts in his diary from 1923: "Every evening, after dinner, we gather around the kitchen table. Grandfather teaches the younger ones the art of carving, passing on not only a technique, but also stories and legends that make each figurine a unique piece of family history."

The 20th century saw alternating periods of decline and rebirth of Christmas craftsmanship. During the world wars, the need to save and the scarcity of commercial goods led to a forced return to the handmade. Many grandmothers still remember how, during these difficult times, the most precious gifts were precisely those made with recycled materials, full of emotional meaning.

During the years of the economic boom, the culture of consumerism seemed to have definitively supplanted that of craftsmanship. Yet, just when the shops began to fill up with standardized products, the first resistance movements arose. In 1968, a group of craftsmen in Copenhagen published the "Manifesto of Conscious Gifting", which criticized the commercialization of Christmas and proposed a return to craftsmanship as a form of cultural resistance.

Today, we are witnessing a true renaissance of the handmade, fueled by several factors. Growing environmental awareness has led many people to reconsider the value of handmade objects as an alternative to unbridled consumerism. Social media has created global communities of makers who share techniques and inspiration. Pinterest reports that searches for "handmade Christmas gifts" have increased by 317% in the last five years.

But there is something deeper behind this return to craftsmanship. As psychologist Sofia Bianchi explains: "Making a gift with your own hands is an act of care that goes beyond the material value of the object. It is a way to dedicate time and attention to someone, in an era in which both have become precious goods."

New technologies, paradoxically, are playing a key role in this renaissance. 3D printers and laser cutters have democratized artisanal production, allowing anyone to create personalized objects. But it's not just about technology: Christmas markets dedicated to artisanal crafts are experiencing a new golden age. The Salzburg market, one of the oldest in Europe, has seen the number of stalls dedicated exclusively to handmade crafts triple in the last ten years.

Emma Thompson, a teacher from Manchester, has been running Christmas craft workshops for her students for five years. "When children create something with their hands," she says, "they learn that the value of a gift is not measured in money. They see how a piece of fabric or wood can be transformed into something special through their creativity and effort."

The tradition of handmade gifts is also influencing the way companies approach the holiday market. More and more brands are incorporating elements of personalization and craftsmanship into their offerings. As third-generation artisan Marco Rossi observes: "People are no longer looking for just objects, they are looking for stories. They want gifts that have a soul, that speak of the person who created them and the person who will receive them."

The return to the handmade is therefore much more than a simple trend: it is a return to the deepest roots of Christmas gift-giving, a way to reconnect with that tradition of care and attention that Saint Nicholas embodied. In an increasingly digital and standardized world, the rediscovery of craftsmanship reminds us that the true value of a gift lies not in its price, but in the love and attention with which it is created.

CHAPTER 9: SANTA CLAUS AND SPIRITUALITY

THE MESSAGE OF LOVE AND GENEROSITY: THE SPIRITUAL LEGACY OF ST. NICHOLAS

On the cold night of December 6, 1917, in a trench on the Western Front, something extraordinary happened. German and British soldiers, separated by a few meters of no man's land, began exchanging small gifts through the barbed wire. A German soldier, Karl Schmidt, wrote in his diary: "Today is the feast of St. Nicholas. We shared our bread with the enemy, just as the saint taught us. For a moment, the war seemed very far away."

This little-known but well-documented episode in military archives perfectly illustrates how the spiritual message of St. Nicholas has survived through the centuries, transcending borders, wars and cultural differences. The spiritual legacy of the Bishop of Myra goes far beyond the miracles and legends that surround him: it is a universal message of love and generosity that continues to resonate even in our time.

The writings of Methodius, Patriarch of Constantinople in the ninth century, offer one of the first reflections on the spiritual dimension of Nicholas' work: "It was not so much the miracles that made this man extraordinary, but his ability to see Christ in every person in need." This spiritual vision of charity as a manifestation of divine love has profoundly shaped the way in which the figure of Saint Nicholas has been perceived and transmitted.

In 1223, St. Francis of Assisi, visiting the crypt of St. Nicholas in Bari, wrote a letter to his brothers: "I have seen today how the common people venerate this saint, not for his miracles, but for his humility in giving. He did not seek glory, but gave in secret, as every true follower of Christ should do." This Franciscan interpretation of the message of St. Nicholas has contributed significantly to shaping the most intimate and spiritual aspect of his legacy.

During the time of the Protestant Reformation, when many saint cults were questioned, the figure of Saint Nicholas retained his peculiar universality. Martin Luther himself, while criticizing the cult of saints, wrote in 1530: "If there is an example that shows how true faith manifests itself in works, it is Nicholas of Myra. He did not only preach love, he lived it."

Anthropologist Viktor Schenk, in his 1892 study "The Spirit of Giving", documents how in European rural communities the figure of Saint Nicholas was associated not so much with miracles as with the concept of the "heilige Pflicht" (sacred duty) of sharing. Interviewing elderly farmers in Bavaria, Schenk collected surprising testimonies: "For us, Saint Nicholas was not so much a miracle worker as an example of how we should live every day. When we share our bread with the hungry, we become a little like him."

The transition from saint to secular figure has not erased this profound spiritual message. In 1875, Victorian writer Elizabeth Gaskell observed: "It is curious how, though he has lost much of his religious connotation, Father Christmas continues to embody so perfectly the Christian virtues of charity and love of fellow man." This observation captures a fundamental aspect of St. Nicholas's spiritual legacy: his ability to communicate universal values even in an increasingly secularized context.

Children's letters to Santa Claus, preserved in postal archives in various countries, offer a touching testimony to how this spiritual message continues to resonate. In 1934, a little girl from Manchester wrote: "Dear Santa Claus, I don't want any toys this year. Could you help my mother who is ill instead? I know you are not God, but perhaps you can do something." This letter shows how, in the popular imagination, the figure of Santa Claus retains the dimension of spiritual intercessor that was typical of Saint Nicholas.

Rabbi David Cohen, in a 1952 essay titled "The Universal Saint," writes: "It is significant how the figure of St. Nicholas/Santa Claus has managed to maintain a profound spiritual message across religions and cultures. He is no longer just a Christian saint, but a universal symbol of what in Jewish tradition we call tzedakah - justice manifested through charity."

Contemporary sociological studies confirm this persistence of the spiritual message. Research conducted in 2015 by Professor Maria Contini of the University of Bologna on a sample of families of different religious faiths revealed how the figure of Santa Claus is used by parents of different confessions to transmit universal spiritual values such as generosity and empathy.

A particularly telling example comes from Japan, where Christmas is not a traditional religious holiday. Historian Takashi Yamamoto documents how, after World War II, many Buddhist schools incorporated the figure of Santa Claus into their spiritual teaching, seeing him as an example of a "contemporary bodhisattva" - a being who dedicates his existence to the good of others.

In 2008, during the financial crisis, a group of Wall Street bankers created the "Saint Nicholas Project", inspired by the example of the saint: each participant committed to anonymously donate part of their bonus to families in difficulty. As one of the founders explained:

"We have rediscovered the true meaning of giving through the example of Saint Nicholas. It is not about ostentatious charity, but about true sharing."

The spiritual legacy of Saint Nicholas continues to evolve and find new forms of expression. On social media, the hashtag #BeASaintNicholas has gone viral, inspiring people around the world to perform anonymous acts of kindness. As sociologist Jennifer Martinez observes, "It's fascinating to see how a spiritual message born in the third century finds new forms of expression in the digital age, while keeping its essence intact."

In today's world, where materialism seems to dominate the Christmas season, the spiritual message of St. Nicholas emerges with renewed force. It is no longer tied to a specific religious denomination, but speaks a universal language of love and generosity that continues to touch the hearts of people of every culture and belief.

RELIGIOUS TRADITIONS: HOW CHRISTMAS IS CELEBRATED IN DIFFERENT CONFESSIONS

In the winter of 1843, something extraordinary happened in a small Coptic church in Cairo. The Orthodox patriarch and the imam of the local mosque gathered together to celebrate what contemporary documents call "The Feast of Shared Light." As the diary of a Venetian merchant present that evening recounts: "Never would I have imagined that Christians and Muslims would gather around the figure of a saint. And yet, the story of Saint Nicholas seemed to speak to them all equally."

This historical episode introduces us to one of the most fascinating aspects of the figure of Saint Nicholas: his ability to cross confessional boundaries. A 12th-century Arabic manuscript, preserved in the library of Alexandria, describes how local Muslims venerated "Al-Qiddis Nikula" (Saint Nicholas) as a holy man, although they did not consider him a saint in the Christian sense of the term.

Russian Orthodox tradition offers one of the richest interpretations of the religious significance of St. Nicholas. Metropolitan Hilarion of Kiev, in a sermon in 1051, wrote: "Nikolai is not just a saint to be venerated, but a model of how divinity manifests itself through concrete acts of mercy." This vision has profoundly influenced the way Eastern churches have integrated the figure of St. Nicholas into their liturgical practices.

The case of the Armenian community in Jerusalem is particularly interesting. The archives of the Armenian Patriarchate preserve a document from 1375 that describes a unique ceremony: during the feast of St. Nicholas, believers brought gifts not only to Christian children, but also to Muslim and Jewish children in the neighborhood. Patriarch Mesrop II commented: "In this way we honor the true nature of the saint, who did not distinguish between the people he helped."

In the Protestant world, the relationship with Saint Nicholas has followed a complex and fascinating path. During the Reformation, many Protestant communities tried to eliminate the cult of saints, but the figure of Saint Nicholas proved surprisingly resilient. A Lutheran pastor from Hamburg wrote in his diary in 1647: "As much as we try to purify the faith from saints, the people continue to see in Nicholas something different, not an intermediary with God, but an example of how to live the faith through works."

The Quaker community in Philadelphia offers a particularly interesting example of how different religious traditions have reinterpreted the figure of St. Nicholas. In 1789, Elizabeth Fry, a prominent Quaker, wrote: "Though we do not venerate saints, we recognize in this ancient story a truth that transcends religious divisions: the divine light manifests itself through acts of disinterested love."

In the Jewish world, the figure of St. Nicholas has found unexpected echoes. Rabbi Mordechai Kaplan, in his "Judaism as a Civilization" (1934), noted how many Jewish families had adapted some aspects of the tradition of St. Nicholas to their own religious practices: "It is not so much the figure of the saint that is embraced as the principle of tzedakah (justice/charity) that he embodied."

Coptic communities in Egypt have maintained a particularly rich tradition associated with Saint Nicholas. A manuscript from the monastery of Saint Macarius, dated 1412, describes elaborate celebrations in which the story of the saint was told through songs in three languages: Coptic, Arabic, and Greek. The text emphasizes how this linguistic plurality symbolized the universality of the saint's message.

In modern African churches, the figure of St. Nicholas has undergone interesting transformations. Archbishop Desmond Tutu, in a sermon in 1986, said: "In our Ubuntu tradition, where each person's humanity is linked to that of others, the story of St. Nicholas takes on a special meaning. He is no longer just a European saint, but becomes a symbol of human interconnectedness."

Christian communities in India have developed their own interpretation of Saint Nicholas. A document from the Syro-Malabar Church of Kerala, dating back to 1892, describes how the figure of the saint was integrated with elements of local spirituality: "For us, Nicholas is like a Christian sadhu, a saint who has renounced material wealth to serve others."

In the Greek Orthodox world, the celebration of Saint Nicholas maintains a strong maritime character. The Metropolitan of Piraeus, in a pastoral letter of 1923, wrote: "For us Greeks, Nicholas is not only the protector of children, but above all the saint who protects those who go to sea. In him we see a bridge between the divine and the human, between land and water."

The Roman Catholic Church, while standardizing many aspects of the cult of St. Nicholas, has maintained a remarkable diversity of local traditions. The Vatican archives preserve accounts of unique celebrations in different parts of the world. An 1856 report from the Catholic mission in Alaska describes how the Yupik natives had integrated St. Nicholas into their traditional beliefs, seeing him as a benevolent spirit who traveled between worlds.

Christian communities in the Middle East offer a particular example of how the figure of Saint Nicholas can serve as an interreligious bridge. A document from the Maronite Patriarchate from 1897 describes common celebrations between Christians and Druze in Lebanon, where the figure of the saint was honored as a symbol of universal wisdom and generosity.

In the contemporary world, this plurality of religious interpretations continues to evolve. As theologian Catherine Bell observes in her 2012 study: "The figure of Saint Nicholas/Santa Claus represents a rare example of how a religious symbol can transcend its confessional origins to become a meeting point between different spiritual traditions."

REFLECTIONS ON THE SACRED: THE SPIRITUAL MEANING OF CHRISTMAS TODAY

Over the centuries, the spiritual meaning of Christmas has undergone profound transformations, yet it maintains its ability to touch the deepest chords of the human soul. In an era characterized by rapid social and technological changes, it is worth asking what the true spiritual meaning of this holiday is and how the figure of Santa Claus fits into this broader context.

"The sacred does not disappear, it transforms," wrote French sociologist Henri Desroche in 1957, and this reflection finds particular resonance when analyzing the evolution of the spiritual meaning of Christmas in contemporary society. In a 2018 study conducted by the University of Milan-Bicocca on a sample of Italian families, it emerged that 78% of participants consider Christmas primarily as a moment of spiritual connection, regardless of their religious beliefs.

The figure of Santa Claus, far from being a mere commercial symbol, today embodies a form of spirituality that transcends religious barriers. In a 1992 interview, religious historian Mircea Eliade emphasized that "religious symbols never die, they transform and adapt to new social realities." This observation applies perfectly to the figure of Santa Claus, who has evolved from a Christian saint to a universal symbol of generosity and hope.

A particularly interesting aspect emerges from the analysis of letters sent to Santa Claus. In 2019, a group of researchers from Uppsala University examined over 10,000 letters from children of different nationalities. What struck the scholars was not so much the request for material gifts, but rather the emergence of a sort of "secular prayer". Children turn to Santa Claus as a spiritual figure capable of listening to their deepest concerns, their wishes for family peace, healing for sick relatives, happiness for their loved ones.

Professor Maria Contini, a cultural anthropologist at the University of Bologna, has documented a particular phenomenon in multicultural communities: families of different religious faiths participate in Christmas celebrations, recognizing them as a moment of spiritual sharing that goes beyond doctrinal differences. "It is as if Santa Claus has become a bridge between different forms of spirituality," the scholar states in her 2020 research notes.

A prime example of this spiritual transformation can be found in the small town of Rovaniemi, Finland, which is considered the official home of Santa Claus. The Santa Claus Village opened there in 1985 and has since evolved into a secular sanctuary. Visitors come not just for fun, but often describe the experience as a "modern pilgrimage." As Erik Svensson, a local guide for over 30 years, says: "I've seen people of all faiths get emotional when they meet Santa Claus. It's not just the magic of the moment, it's something deeper, as if they're rediscovering a forgotten part of their spirituality."

The spiritual dimension of contemporary Christmas is also manifested through new ritual forms. In large European and American cities, "Christmas sharing circles" are increasingly widespread, spontaneous groups of people who gather during the holiday season to reflect on the profound meaning of Christmas.

During these meetings, as social psychologist Robert Thompson documents, "people share personal stories related to Christmas, often referring to Santa Claus as a symbol of hope and spiritual renewal."

The relationship between traditional and modern spirituality finds an interesting synthesis in the words of Father Giovanni Bertolini, a Dominican theologian who in 2015 published a study on the contemporary meaning of Christmas: "The figure of Santa Claus does not replace the religious meaning of Christmas, but enriches it with new meanings. It is as if society had found in this character a way to express its need for transcendence in more accessible and universal forms".

A particularly significant phenomenon emerged during the 2020 pandemic, when many families, unable to celebrate Christmas in the traditional ways, rediscovered more intimate and spiritual dimensions of the holiday. Video calls with Santa Claus, initially conceived as a surrogate for traditional visits, transformed into moments of deep emotional and spiritual connection.

The spirituality of contemporary Christmas is also manifested through concrete gestures of solidarity. More and more people choose to dedicate the Christmas period to volunteering, embodying the spirit of generosity that first Saint Nicholas, and then Santa Claus, have represented over the centuries. As American sociologist Jennifer Martinez observes: "The true miracle of modern Christmas is its ability to inspire concrete actions of help towards others, transforming a spiritual symbol into social practice".

The spiritual meaning of Christmas today has not been lost, but has transformed, adapting to the needs of an increasingly complex and multicultural society. Santa Claus, far from being a simple commercial character, has become the guardian of a modern spirituality that, while maintaining ties with tradition, knows how to speak to the hearts of people of every culture and religious belief. As an ancient Finnish proverb recalls: "The most precious gift is not the one found under the tree, but the one discovered in one's heart".

SANTA CLAUS AS A SYMBOL OF HOPE: THE SOCIAL IMPACT OF HIS STORIES

In the cold streets of Berlin in 1948, during the difficult times of the Soviet blockade, something extraordinary happened. American pilot Hal Halvorsen, who was flying an airlift to supply the isolated city, noticed a group of children watching the planes through the barbed wire at Tempelhof Airport. Moved by compassion, he promised to drop candy from his plane the next day, signaling his arrival by flapping his wings. He soon became known as "Uncle Wiggly Wings" and "The Candy Bomber." This rarely told story perfectly illustrates how the figure of Santa Claus can embody hope even in the darkest moments of history.

"Hope dies last," goes the old proverb, and few figures in modern history have embodied this concept like Santa Claus. Over the years, this figure has become a powerful catalyst for social change and a bearer of hope in surprisingly diverse contexts.

During the Great Depression of the 1930s, when American families were struggling to survive, a peculiar tradition arose in New York police stations. Officers, dressed as Santa Claus, would distribute not only toys but also basic necessities to families in need. As social historian Mary Thompson recounted in her 1934 diaries: "It wasn't just a matter of giving presents, it was a way of telling people that they hadn't been forgotten, that there was still hope."

A particularly poignant example of Santa's social impact comes from a 1995 study at Boston Children's Hospital. Dr. Sarah Martinez documented how terminally ill children found comfort not in material gifts but in the figure of Santa Claus as a symbol of continuity and hope. "For these children," Martinez writes, "Santa Claus represented something that would continue after they were gone, a link between the present and a future they would never see."

In 1963, in the midst of the Cold War, NORAD (North American Aerospace Defense Command) accidentally began tracking Santa Claus on Christmas Eve. What began as a typo in a local newspaper—which printed the number of the military command instead of that of a store offering Santa calls—turned into a tradition that still unites millions of people around the world. Colonel Harry Shoup, who received the first call from a child that night, decided to play along rather than explain the mistake. As he recalled years later, "I realized that Santa could be a bridge between seemingly irreconcilable worlds."

Santa Claus stories of social impact aren't limited to the Western world. In 1982, in a small Japanese village suffering from a severe economic crisis, a group of elderly people began dressing up as Santa Claus to visit children's homes not just at Christmas, but throughout the year. The initiative, documented by anthropologist Takashi Yamamoto, led to a surprising result: "The school dropout rate dropped dramatically. Children saw these 'Santa Clauses' as role models, who encouraged them not to give up despite the difficulties."

A particularly significant aspect of Santa's social impact emerges from the analysis of letters preserved at the Rovaniemi Postal Archive. Professor Elena Rossi, who studied over 50,000 letters sent between 1960 and 2020, identified an interesting pattern: "While in times of economic prosperity the requests are mainly material, during crises the letters reveal a deeper desire for human connection and collective hope."

In 2008, during the global financial crisis, a significant phenomenon emerged: the number of volunteers offering to play Santa Claus in underserved communities increased by 300%. As sociologist James Parker observed: "It was as if people felt the need to actively embody the hope that Santa Claus represents, rather than simply be spectators."

Santa's social impact is also manifested through innovative initiatives. In 2015, a group of Seattle-based programmers created "Santa's Hope Network," a platform that connects families in need with anonymous donors throughout the year. As founder Maria Chen explains: "We wanted to extend Santa's spirit beyond the holidays, creating an ongoing support system based on the same idea of anonymous generosity and hope."

A particularly touching story emerged from a refugee camp in Greece in 2016. A group of volunteers, noticing the desperation of Syrian children, organized an impromptu Christmas celebration. An eight-year-old girl, interviewed by a local journalist, said: "I didn't know Santa Claus before, but now I know he represents the hope that one day we can return home." This testimony highlights how the symbol of Santa Claus can transcend cultural and religious barriers to become a universal messenger of hope.

In the contemporary world, Santa's social impact is also manifested through social justice initiatives. In 2019, a group of activists in Melbourne created "Santa's Social Justice Network", an organization that uses the figure of Santa to raise awareness on issues such as child poverty and access to education. As founder David Thompson says: "Santa is not just a giver of gifts, but a symbol of social equity and hope for a better world."

The power of Santa Claus as a symbol of hope was especially evident during the 2020 pandemic. When traditional visits to Santa Claus at the mall became impossible, new forms of connection emerged. Video calls with Santa, initially seen as a stopgap, revealed unexpected potential. As child psychologist Laura Bennett notes, "The intimacy of these virtual meetings allowed for deeper, more meaningful conversations. Children talked not just about gifts, but about fears, hopes, and dreams for the future."

CHAPTER 10: THE SYMBOLS OF CHRISTMAS

THE CHRISTMAS TREE: ORIGINS AND MEANING

On the night of December 24, 1832, Princess Helene of Mecklenburg-Schwerin, newly married to the Duke of Orleans, son of Louis-Philippe of France, introduced for the first time to the Tuileries a tradition that would forever change the face of French Christmas. In the middle of the main hall of the palace, she erected a majestic fir tree decorated with candles and candied fruit, arousing wonder and amazement among the aristocrats present. That evening, without knowing it, the German princess was contributing to the spread of one of the oldest and most fascinating Christmas traditions in history.

The history of the Christmas tree has its roots in a past much more remote than one might imagine. In 723 AD, Saint Boniface was in the lands of pagan Germany, intent on his work of evangelization. According to legend, he came across a group of druids who were about to sacrifice a young man near an oak tree sacred to Thor. With a blow of his axe, the saint cut down the tree, and in its place a small fir tree miraculously grew. "This little tree," he told those present, "with its evergreen leaves, represents the eternal life promised by Christ."

Archaeologists have discovered even older traces of this tradition. In 2018, during excavations near Uppsala, Sweden, remains of plant decorations dating back to the Viking period were found. Professor Ingrid Johansson, head of the excavations, documented how "the ancient Nordic people decorated evergreen trees during the winter solstice, hanging amulets and offerings to the gods to celebrate the return of light."

In the 16th century, in the city of Riga, Latvia, an event occurred that would be passed down through the centuries. The Brotherhood of Blackheads, an association of single merchants, decided to celebrate Christmas by erecting a huge fir tree in the market square and decorating it with ribbons and paper flowers. At the end of the celebrations, the tree was burned, but before doing so, each member of the brotherhood had to dance around it and then jump through the flames, a ritual that combined pagan and Christian elements.

A particularly interesting document, preserved in the Strasbourg archives, dates back to 1605. It is the diary of a merchant who describes with wonder the Christmas trees he had seen in the city: "In Strasbourg, they bring fir trees into the houses and decorate them with colored paper roses, apples, wafers, tinsel and sweets". This text represents one of the first written testimonies of the domestic use of the Christmas tree as we know it today.

The tradition of the Christmas tree took a significant turn in 1848, when the Illustrated London News published an engraving of Queen Victoria and Prince Albert with their children around a decorated tree in Windsor Castle. As historian Simon Jenkins recalls: "That single image did more for the popularization of the Christmas tree than any other event in British history. Suddenly, every middle-class family wanted to have their own tree."

In the Germanic world, the tradition had developed unique characteristics. In Nuremberg, in the 17th century, trees were decorated with what was called "angel bread", thin colored wafers that represented the Eucharistic bread. As a parish register from 1657 documents: "For each Christmas tree in the church, twelve wafers are used, to remember the apostles, and a larger one at the top, to symbolize Christ".

A little-known fact concerns the evolution of decorations. In 1847, a glassblower from Lauscha, Thuringia, named Hans Greiner, created the first glass Christmas tree ornaments. Legend has it that he was too poor to afford the traditional apples and nuts, so he decided to use the material he knew best. His innovation was an immediate success, so much so that in 1880 F.W. Woolworth began importing Lauscha ornaments to the United States, starting a business that would generate a fortune.

The candles on the tree, now replaced by the safer electric lights, have a peculiar history. In 1882, Edward Johnson, a colleague of Thomas Edison, created the first set of electric Christmas lights. As the Detroit Post and Tribune reported at the time: "Mr. Johnson lit a Christmas tree with eighty small electric lights about the size of a walnut, creating a display of rare beauty that drew a crowd of onlookers to his house."

The Great Depression of the 1930s left an interesting mark on the history of the Christmas tree. During this time, many families could not afford expensive decorations, and so the tradition of the "friendship tree" was born. Families would exchange handmade ornaments, often made from recycled materials. As Mary Thompson wrote in her 1934 diary, "Our tree this year is decorated with newspaper stars and button garlands. Each ornament tells a story of friendship and togetherness."

A fascinating chapter concerns Christmas trees during times of war. During World War I, on the battlefields, soldiers from both sides created makeshift Christmas trees in the trenches. German soldier Kurt Schmidt wrote in his diary on Christmas Eve 1914: "We decorated a small fir tree with candles and some objects found in our backpacks. For a moment, looking at that tree, the war seemed far away."

The ecological aspect of the Christmas tree has an interesting history. In 1901, American conservationist Franklin Pierce first suggested the idea of specially grown Christmas trees. In his pamphlet "The Christmas Tree Question," he wrote: "We do not have to choose between tradition and the preservation of our forests. We can have both by planning and growing the trees we need."

In the contemporary world, the Christmas tree continues to evolve. In 2019, Japanese artist Yayoi Kusama created a completely digital Christmas tree in London, projected onto the façade of the Tate Modern. As art critic Sarah Wilson commented: "The Christmas tree is changing along with our society, but it retains its profound meaning of rebirth and hope."

The Christmas tree represents much more than a simple festive decoration. It is a symbol that has crossed centuries of history, cultures and different traditions, adapting and transforming, but always maintaining its deepest meaning of life, rebirth and hope. As the German poet Rainer Maria Rilke wrote in 1902: "The Christmas tree is like a bridge between heaven and earth, a living symbol that reminds us that even in the heart of winter, life continues to pulsate".

THE CHRISTMAS STAR: SYMBOLISM AND TRADITIONS RELATED TO THE COMET STAR

In the firmament of Christmas symbols, the star shines with a special light, guiding not only the Three Wise Men to Bethlehem but also the collective imagination throughout the centuries. Its constant presence in Christmas representations, from nativity scenes to modern decorations, tells a story that intertwines astronomy, faith and popular folklore.

On the evening of December 24, 7 BC, an extraordinary astronomical event lit up the skies of the Middle East. The Babylonian astronomical archives, preserved on cuneiform tablets and rediscovered only in the 20th century, document a very rare alignment between Jupiter and Saturn in the constellation of Pisces. Professor Werner Keller, in his study "The Star of the Magi", hypothesizes that this planetary conjunction could have been the famous comet described in the Gospel of Matthew. The Magi, wise astronomers of ancient Persia, would have interpreted this phenomenon as the sign of the birth of a predestined king.

"And the star which they had seen in the East went before them, until it came and stood over where the young child was." This passage from the Gospel has fueled centuries of debate among astronomers, theologians and historians. In 1603, the astronomer Johannes Kepler, observing a similar planetary conjunction, was the first to propose a scientific explanation for the phenomenon of the Star of Bethlehem. His observations, published in the treatise "De Stella Nova", represent one of the first attempts to reconcile the biblical narrative with modern astronomy.

But the Christmas star is not just an astronomical phenomenon. In European folk traditions of the Middle Ages, it became a powerful symbol of hope and spiritual guidance. In Germany, the "Stern von Bethlehem" was represented in Christmas processions with elaborate star-shaped lanterns, a tradition that survives to this day at the Christmas markets of Nuremberg. Children, led by the "Sternträger" (star bearer), would march through the streets singing ancient songs such as "Stern über Bethlehem":

"Star over Bethlehem, show us the way, lead us to the stable, where the divine child lies. You, our guide, do not abandon us, until we have reached our goal."

In Scandinavian folklore, the star takes on even more mystical connotations. Ancient Norwegian tales tell of the "Stjernegutt" (the star boy), a young shepherd who, following a particular star in the winter sky, discovered a secret passage to the world of nature spirits. This legend later merged with Christian traditions, creating a fascinating cultural syncretism that still characterizes Christmas celebrations in the Nordic countries today.

The tradition of placing a star on top of the Christmas tree has relatively recent origins. It was introduced in Germany in the 18th century, when Christmas trees began to spread in bourgeois homes. The star represented not only the Star of Bethlehem, but also the divine light that illuminates the path of humanity. An old German proverb says: "Wenn der Stern am Baum erstrahlt, ist das Christkind nicht mehr weit" (When the star shines on the tree, the Baby Jesus is not far away).

In Italy, the tradition of the star is intertwined with that of nativity scenes. Saint Francis of Assisi, in the first living nativity scene in history created in Greccio in 1223, wanted a star-shaped lantern to illuminate the Nativity scene. In documents of the time, Fra Tommaso da Celano describes how "a celestial light seemed to descend from the star, illuminating not only the nativity scene, but also the hearts of those present".

Symbolic interpretations of the Christmas star vary greatly among Christian cultures. In Russian Orthodox tradition, the star represents the eye of God watching over humanity during the Holy Night. An ancient 15th-century icon, preserved in a Novgorod monastery, shows the Star of Bethlehem as an eye surrounded by golden rays, an image that has profoundly influenced Eastern Christmas iconography.

In the 19th century, with the advent of the first industrial Christmas decorations, the Star of Bethlehem became a central element of Christmas merchandising. Woolworth's, a famous American department store chain, commissioned the first blown glass stars from the Lauscha manufactory in Germany in 1880. These ornaments, initially very expensive and considered luxury items, gradually democratized the symbol of the star, bringing it into the homes of millions of families.

A curious tradition related to the Christmas star still survives today in the Philippines. During Advent, villages organize the "Parol", a festival of star lanterns. These elaborate artifacts, originally made of rice paper and bamboo, are now made of modern materials and illuminated by multicolored LEDs. Tradition dictates that each family creates its own star lantern, a symbol of hope and community unity.

The Christmas star has also inspired numerous works of art and musical compositions. In 1918, Norwegian composer Marcus Møller Thrane wrote "Stjernesang" (The Song of the Star), a Christmas cantata that narrates the journey of the Magi from the point of view of the guiding star. The rarely performed but extraordinarily beautiful work captures the magic and mystery of that ancient night:

"Through winds and storms, over mountains and seas, my light guides seekers of truth. I am but a point in the infinite sky, yet within me shines the divine promise."

In the modern world, the Christmas star continues to evolve as a symbol. Contemporary astrophysicists, while proposing scientific explanations for the phenomenon of the Star of Bethlehem (from Halley's Comet to a supernova), recognize the evocative power of this symbol that unites science and spirituality. As astronomer David Hughes wrote in his essay "The Star of Bethlehem Mystery": "The real magic of the Christmas star lies not so much in its astronomical nature as in its ability to inspire wonder and hope generation after generation."

The star thus remains a bridge between heaven and earth, between the material and the spiritual, between science and faith. As it shines silently above our homes during the Christmas season, it continues to remind us that, like the Magi two thousand years ago, we too are on a journey, guided by a light that promises to lead us toward something greater than ourselves.

MISTLETOE AND PINE: BOTANICAL TRADITIONS AT CHRISTMAS

In the heart of winter, when nature seems to be asleep under a blanket of snow, two plants stand as perennial symbols of life that continues: mistletoe and pine. Their presence in Christmas celebrations is not accidental, but is rooted in millennia of history and traditions that intertwine like the branches of these extraordinary plants.

In ancient Britain, Druids considered mistletoe a sacred plant, capable of curing illnesses and bringing fertility. During the winter solstice, Celtic priests would climb ancient oak trees to harvest the evergreen plant with golden sickles, while the people waited beneath the tree to gather the precious sprigs in white linen cloths, preventing them from touching the ground. "The mistletoe that grows between heaven and earth," wrote Pliny the Elder in his Naturalis Historia in the first century AD, "is considered by the Gauls to be a divine emanation." The belief that it brought peace and prosperity was so ingrained that, according to medieval chronicles, when enemies met under a mistletoe branch, they would lay down their weapons and declare a truce for the following day.

The pine tree, on the other hand, tells a different but equally fascinating story. In the 8th century, St. Boniface came across a sacred oak dedicated to Thor near Geismar, Germany. According to Willibald's "Vita Bonifatii," the saint cut down the tree to demonstrate the superiority of Christianity over pagan beliefs. When the oak tree fell, it split into four pieces, and a young pine tree miraculously grew behind it. Boniface took the opportunity to use the tree's triangular shape as a symbol of the Trinity, thus transforming an element of nature into a powerful tool for evangelization.

The tradition of decorating pine branches during the Christmas season finds evocative testimony in a 1494 manuscript preserved in Riga, Latvia. The document describes how merchants from the Brotherhood of Blackheads would decorate a pine tree with silk roses, ribbons, and dried fruit, then dance around it and burn it. "It is as if the tree itself were celebrating with us," the text reads, "its green needles defying winter are a reminder of eternal life."

The botanical properties of these plants have contributed to their sacredness. Mistletoe, with its ability to grow suspended between heaven and earth, seems to defy the laws of nature. Its particular biology, as a semi-parasitic plant, has fueled legends and superstitions. In Nordic folklore, mistletoe was considered the sacred plant of Frigg, the goddess of love. When her son Baldr was killed by a mistletoe arrow, his tears turned into the plant's white berries. Since then, Frigg has blessed with a kiss anyone who passes under the mistletoe, originating the modern tradition of kissing under this lucky branch.

The pine tree, with its evergreen needles, represented for many ancient cultures the victory of life over death. The Romans decorated their homes with pine branches during the Saturnalia, a festival that coincided with the winter solstice. A document from 63 AD, found in the excavations of Herculaneum, describes how "pine branches perfume homes and remind us that even in the heart of winter, nature never completely dies."

The traditions associated with these plants have evolved over time, but have maintained a profound meaning. In the Middle Ages, hanging mistletoe on the front door was not just a decorative gesture, but a ritual of protection. It was believed that the plant could keep evil spirits and witches away. A 12th-century herbal, compiled in the monastery of Monte Cassino, reports that "mistletoe blessed on Christmas night has the power to drive away demons and protect the house from all evil."

The connection between these plants and Christmas has been further strengthened through numerous folk legends. A story spread throughout Central Europe tells of how, on Christmas night, the trees bow toward Bethlehem. Only the pine, because of its faithfulness, remains upright to watch over the sleeping world. An old German ballad from the 15th century, found in the archives of Nuremberg, sings: "The pine stands upright in the holy night, while all the other trees bow toward the star."

The medicinal properties of these plants have contributed to their cultural importance. Mistletoe was used in traditional medicine to treat epilepsy and other neurological conditions. A 1772 medical treatise by Dr. Johann Friedrich von Cronstadt documents the use of mistletoe as a "divine medicine," prescribing it to "calm the agitated nerves and bring peace to the troubled heart." This dual nature of mistletoe, as both a medicinal and symbolic plant, has contributed to its persistence in Christmas traditions.

Pine also has its healing properties. Pine resin was used to make ointments and remedies for respiratory ailments. A 16th century recipe book, preserved in the library of the University of Padua, describes how "pine essence, collected on Christmas night, has particularly beneficial properties, almost as if the sanctity of the moment increased its natural virtues".

Over the centuries, these botanical traditions became intertwined with the figure of Saint Nicholas and later Santa Claus. In parts of Northern Europe, Saint Nicholas was believed to use a pine staff to find the homes of good children, while mistletoe was believed to bless the homes he visited. This association helped cement the role of these plants in Christmas celebrations, transforming them from pagan symbols to integral elements of the Christian holiday.

As we hang mistletoe on our doors and decorate our Christmas pines, we are unknowingly perpetuating age-old traditions that speak of hope, renewal, and the continuity of life.

CHRISTMAS DECORATIONS: EVOLUTION AND MEANING OF THE VARIOUS SYMBOLS

Deep in a glass mine in Thuringia in 1847, a glassblower named Hans Greiner watched anxiously as the last furnace slowly died. The region was experiencing a severe shortage of apples, traditionally used to decorate Christmas trees. In a moment of desperate creativity, Greiner decided to blow glass spheres that mimicked the shape of the missing fruit. Little did he know that he was about to start a revolution in Christmas decorations.

The first Christmas decorations, however, did not originate in the 19th century, but have roots in much more remote times. A Benedictine manuscript from 1171, preserved in the Abbey of Sankt Gallen, describes how the monks "hung small mirrors on the vaults of the church that reflected the light of the candles, creating a starry sky on earth". This medieval practice represents one of the first documented attempts to create a Christmas atmosphere through decorative elements.

The tradition of light decorations finds interesting evidence in a document from 1660, preserved in the archives of the city of Riga. The city chronicler describes how "the merchants of the Hanseatic League illuminated their houses with candles placed in colored glass containers, transforming the dark streets into paths of multicolored light". This custom quickly spread throughout Northern Europe, where artificial light took on a special meaning during the long winter nights.

In the 16th century, Christmas decorations took on a deeper meaning in the homes of Protestant Reformed Christians. Martin Luther himself, in a 1536 letter to his wife Katharina von Bora, describes how "the little lights on the tree remind children of the stars in the sky under which the Savior was born." This testimony reveals how decorative elements were not merely aesthetic frivolities, but bearers of profound spiritual meanings.

Golden pine cones, still popular Christmas decorations today, have a special history. An inventory of the Medici residence in Florence, dated 1587, lists "twelve pine cones covered in gold leaf, to be used in the celebrations of Holy Christmas." Pine cones, a symbol of fertility in classical antiquity, were transformed into precious ornaments that united pagan and Christian traditions.

The history of Christmas decorations takes a significant turn in the 18th century. In 1739, Princess Victoria von Schwarzburg-Rudolstadt introduced a revolutionary innovation: she ordered her craftsmen to create blown glass decorations in the shape of angels and stars. Her personal diary, discovered in 1952, reveals how "the fragile glass figures catch the light of the candles so magically that it seems as if the tree is inhabited by celestial beings."

The tradition of colored glass balls evolved rapidly. In 1848, an article in the "Leipziger Illustrierte Zeitung" described Greiner's creations with wonder: "The glass balls are not simple substitutes for apples, but have become miniature works of art, each containing a world of colors and reflections." The production in Lauscha, Greiner's village, became so famous that in 1880 F. W. Woolworth, the great American entrepreneur, crossed the Atlantic especially to import these decorations to the United States.

A fascinating aspect of Christmas decorations is represented by the figures of angels. A document from 1795, from a convent in Salzburg, describes how the nuns "wove silver threads and small glass beads to create angels to hang on the Christmas tree, each with a name and a specific prayer." This tradition of the personalized angel has continued in many families to this day.

Paper decorations have an equally interesting history. In 1816, during the difficult period following the Napoleonic Wars, a Nuremberg teacher, Johanna Spörl, taught her students how to make Christmas decorations out of colored paper. Her notebook, kept in the city museum, contains detailed instructions for making paper stars and chains, accompanied by this touching note: "Even in the darkest times, we can create beauty with our hands."

The introduction of electricity revolutionized the world of Christmas decorations. The first electrically lit Christmas tree was unveiled in 1882 by Edward Johnson, an associate of Thomas Edison. The Detroit Post and Tribune described the event as "a magical spectacle: eighty little red, white, and blue lights that shone like terrestrial stars." This innovation opened up new decorative possibilities, even though electric lights were initially a luxury reserved for the very wealthy.

Christmas decorations have also spanned periods of special historical significance. During World War I, for example, Iron Cross decorations became popular in Germany, while patriotic bunting became popular in England. A moving soldier's diary from 1916 describes how "the decorations on the Christmas tree in the trenches reminded us of home and the hope of peace."

During the 20th century, Christmas decorations were influenced by mass-produced industrial production. However, this did not eliminate the appeal of traditional craftsmanship. A 1952 article in "House & Garden" magazine noted that "despite the availability of mass-produced decorations, many families jealously guard old ornaments passed down from generation to generation, each carrying family stories and memories."

Every ball, every ribbon, every light tells a story that goes far beyond its decorative value, testifying to the human ability to transform simple objects into bearers of deep and lasting meanings.

CHAPTER 11: CHRISTMAS IN CINEMA AND POP CULTURE

ICONIC CHRISTMAS MOVIES: SANTA CLAUS AT THE MOVIES

In the winter of 1898, in a small film studio in Brighton, George Albert Smith was about to make history. His one-minute short film "Santa Claus" was the first time Father Christmas had appeared on the big screen. The film showed the mythical figure coming down a chimney using a crude but innovative double-exposure technique. "I want children to believe that magic is real," Smith wrote in his production diary, now held by the British Film Institute.

The magic of cinema has played a major role in shaping the modern image of Santa Claus, transforming a folkloric character into a universal cultural icon. In 1905, film pioneer Edwin S. Porter made "The Night Before Christmas," the first film adaptation of Clement Clarke Moore's famous poem. A New York Times critic at the time wrote, "Moving pictures have brought to life the words that have filled American children's dreams for generations."

A pivotal moment in the cinematic portrayal of Santa Claus came in 1947 with "Miracle on 34th Street." The film addressed a fundamental question: Can a department store hire the real Santa Claus? Edmund Gwenn, who played Kris Kringle, prepared for the role in a unique way. According to production diaries, the actor spent three weeks working as Santa Claus in a New York department store, without revealing his true identity. "I realized I wasn't playing a character," Gwenn wrote in his memoirs, "I was creating a symbol of hope."

The 1960s saw the emergence of a new television tradition with "Rudolph the Red-Nosed Reindeer" (1964), a stop-motion special that introduced a more complex and multifaceted Santa Claus. Arthur Rankin Jr., the producer, revealed in a 1985 interview, "We wanted to show that even Santa Claus can make mistakes. That makes him more human and, paradoxically, more magical."

A significant shift in perspective came in 1985 with "Santa Claus: The Movie." Director Jeannot Szwarc drew inspiration from creation myths to tell the story of Santa's origins. David Huddleston, who played the title role, spent months studying various Christmas traditions. "In every culture," he said in an interview at the premiere, "I found one common element: the desire to believe in something greater than ourselves."

1994 marked a turning point with "The Santa Clause." Tim Allen played an ordinary man who is forced to become Santa Claus. The film explored a novel concept: What if Santa Claus were a role passed down from person to person? John Pasquin, the director, recalls: "We wanted to democratize the magic of Christmas. Anyone could be called upon to be Santa Claus."

One of the most controversial interpretations came in 2003 with "Bad Santa." Billy Bob Thornton presented an anti-Santa, a cynical and disillusioned character. Terry Zwigoff, the director, defended his vision in an interview with Sight & Sound: "Sometimes we need to look at the darkness to truly appreciate the light. Our film is about redemption, just like the original story of St. Nicholas."

In 2012, "Rise of the Guardians" offered a completely new take on Santa Claus, portraying him as a tattooed warrior with twin swords. Director Peter Ramsey drew inspiration from ancient legends of

Cossack warriors. "I wanted to remind people that St. Nicholas comes from Turkey," he explained in an interview, "and that his story is much older and more complex than we think."

Technology has played a major role in the evolution of the cinematic depiction of Santa Claus. In 2004, "Polar Express" used motion capture to create a digital Santa. Tom Hanks, who played multiple roles in the film, described the experience as "a return to the essence of acting." Director Robert Zemeckis wanted his Santa to feel "real but still magical, tangible but mysterious."

An interesting aspect of the cinematic portrayal of Santa Claus is how different actors have interpreted the role. Richard Attenborough, who played Santa Claus in the 1994 remake of "Miracle on 34th Street," spent weeks in a children's home before filming. "Children don't believe in an interpretation," he wrote in his production notes, "they believe in a truth."

Cinema has also explored different Christmas traditions around the world. In 2010, the Finnish documentary "Joulupukki: The Real Santa Claus" showed how Lapland has appropriated the image of Santa Claus. An elderly Rovaniemi villager recalls: "Before Hollywood created its Santa Claus, we already had our Joulupukki. Now the two have merged into one figure."

Over the years, cinema has helped create what we might call a "visual mythology" of Santa Claus. Each film has added a piece to his legend, enriching it with new meanings and interpretations. As Martin Scorsese observed in a 2015 essay on the history of Christmas cinema: "The silver screen has transformed Santa Claus from a religious symbol to a universal cultural icon, while keeping his message of hope and generosity intact."

The cinematic representation of Santa Claus continues to evolve. As Roger Eber wrote, "The cinema did not invent Santa Claus, but it gave him a voice, a face, and a heart that continues to beat across generations."

SANTA CLAUS IN LITERATURE: BOOKS AND STORIES THAT CONTRIBUTED TO HIS LEGEND

In the vast panorama of world literature, few characters have captured the imagination of writers as much as Santa Claus. His figure, plastic and changeable, has crossed centuries of narrations, enriching itself with nuances and meanings always new.

Charles Dickens, with his 1843 "A Christmas Carol", made one of the most significant contributions to Christmas literature, even if his "Spirit of Christmas Present" was not exactly Santa Claus. However, the description of this jovial giant dressed in green, with a wreath of holly on his head, contributed significantly to the evolution of the image of the quintessential Christmas character. As literary critic GK Chesterton wrote in 1906: "Dickens did not invent Christmas, but he certainly rediscovered it."

The real literary revolution in the representation of Santa Claus, however, came with "A Visit from St. Nicholas", better known as "The Night Before Christmas", published anonymously in the "Troy Sentinel" in 1823. The author, later identified as Clement Clarke Moore, created an image destined to become canonical: "He was plump and chubby, a jolly old elf, and I laughed when I saw him, in spite of myself". These verses definitively transformed St. Nicholas into the "jolly old elf" we know today, establishing details that would become integral to the myth: the sleigh, the reindeer, the entrance through the chimney, even the red color of his suit.

German literary tradition offers an interesting counterpoint with Heinrich Hoffmann's "Struwwelpeter" (1845), where Ruprecht, the stern helper of St. Nicholas, appears. In its pages, we find a more austere version of the character, reflecting the Central European tradition of Christmas. As Jacob Grimm wrote in his studies of German folklore: "Ruprecht is the bridge between the old pagan tradition and the new Christian faith."

The Victorian era saw an explosion of Christmas literature. Harper's Weekly magazine published a series of Christmas poems in 1862 that helped solidify the American image of Santa Claus. One of these, "Christmas Eve" by William Gilmore Simms, described Santa Claus as "the patron saint of childish joy," an image that would become central to later literature.

In 1902, L. Frank Baum, author of The Wizard of Oz, published The Life and Adventures of Santa Claus, the first complete and imaginative biography of the character. The book mixed elements of folklore with an original narrative, explaining how Santa Claus was raised by wood nymphs and learned immortality from the Great Ak, the Master Woodcutter of Life. "In every child lives a spark of divinity," Baum wrote, "and when we give them joy, that spark shines a little brighter."

Russian literature offers a unique perspective with the figure of Ded Moroz, "Grandfather Frost." In Nikolai Nekrasov's poem "Moroz, Krasnyj Nos" (1864), we find a powerful description of this winter figure who, while not strictly speaking Santa Claus, shares many of his attributes. His portrayal greatly influenced Eastern European literature.

In the early 20th century, St. Nicholas Magazine became a major vehicle for Christmas literature. Between 1873 and 1940, it published hundreds of stories that helped define the modern image of Santa Claus. Mary Mapes Dodge, its editor for over thirty years, insisted that every Christmas story should contain "an element of wonder coupled with a solid moral basis."

In 1939, Robert L. May created Rudolph the Red-Nosed Reindeer for Montgomery Ward. What began as a free promotional booklet became a classic of Christmas literature, selling millions of copies and spawning a hit song. May drew on his own experience as a shy and often mocked child, transforming the story into a powerful message of acceptance and redemption.

Contemporary literature has continued to reinterpret the figure of Santa Claus. In 1994, Chris Van Allsburg published "Polar Express," a story that explores the theme of faith and doubt through a magical journey to the North Pole. The book won the Caldecott Medal and became a modern classic, demonstrating how the figure of Santa Claus can still inspire significant literary works.

The 1990s also saw the emergence of more ironic and subversive interpretations. David Sedaris, with his "Holidays on Ice" (1997), presented a satirical view of Santa's world through the eyes of a department store elf. As the New York Times wrote: "Sedaris has done for Santa's elves what Joseph Heller did for war."

The Italian literary tradition has contributed with works such as "Lettere a Babbo Natale" by Gianni Rodari (1962), where the author uses the figure of Santa Claus to address social and pedagogical issues. "Children's letters to Santa Claus", wrote Rodari, "are mirrors of their hopes and fears, but also of the society in which they live".

Terry Pratchett, in his "Santa Claus, Inc." (1996), created a brilliant satire that explores the commercial aspects of Christmas through the lens of humorous fantasy. His version of Santa Claus is a CEO struggling with logistics and marketing problems, while retaining the character's magical essence.

Through these literary examples, we can see how the figure of Santa Claus has evolved from a simple bringer of gifts to a complex symbol of hope, generosity, and magic.

CARTOONS AND SANTA CLAUS: THE INFLUENCE OF THE MEDIA ON THE IMAGE OF SANTA CLAUS

In the universe of animation, Santa Claus has found one of his most vivid and enduring expressions. The world of cartoons has allowed the magic of Christmas to be brought to life in ways that no other medium could have achieved, contributing significantly to the evolution of the image of this character in the collective imagination.

One of the first animated representations of Santa Claus dates back to 1925, with the black-and-white short "The Toy Shop" by Fleischer Studios. During a screening at the time, a New York Times critic wrote, "Animation has given Santa Claus a freedom of movement and an expressiveness that no live actor could ever equal." This pioneering work already showed the potential of animation in capturing the magic of the character.

In 1932, Walt Disney produced "Santa's Workshop," a Silly Symphonies short that was a game-changer. For the first time, audiences could see Santa's workshop in all its animated glory, complete with hard-working elves and dancing toys. As Ward Kimball, one of Disney's Nine Old Men, recalled, "Walt wanted every detail of the workshop to look real and magical at the same time. We spent weeks studying the mechanisms of the toys to make the animations as believable as possible."

The 1940s saw the arrival of Max Fleischer's "Rudolph the Red-Nosed Reindeer." This 1948 short was the precursor to the popular 1964 stop-motion version. Arthur Rankin Jr., who would later co-produce the '64 version, said in a 1985 interview, "The Fleischer short showed us that you could tell a serious Christmas story through animation, without losing the sense of wonder."

The real revolution in Christmas animation came in 1964 with Rankin/Bass Productions' "Rudolph the Red-Nosed Reindeer." Using the stop-motion technique called "Animagic," this television special created a unique aesthetic that would influence generations of artists. Jules Bass recalled, "We wanted the characters to have a tangibility that traditional animation couldn't provide. Every movement had to look real, but still have an element of fantasy."

In 1970, Rankin/Bass produced "Santa Claus Is Comin' to Town," the first animated version of Santa Claus's origin story. Fred Astaire, who voiced the narrator-mailman, commented, "This version of the story gave Santa a backstory that made him more human and relatable to children." The special introduced biographical elements that would become canon, such as the explanation of why Santa Claus comes down chimneys.

Japanese animation offered a unique perspective with "Little Santa Claus" (1984). Character designer Yasuji Mori created a young and dynamic version of the character, influencing how later anime would depict Christmas figures. As he said in an interview, "We wanted to show that Santa Claus was once young and had to learn his trade."

The 1990s brought a breath of fresh air with Tim Burton's "The Nightmare Before Christmas" (1993). Although not technically a traditional animated film, this stop-motion work revolutionized the perception of how Christmas could be represented in animation. Henry Selick, the director, stated, "We wanted to create a world where Christmas was seen through completely different eyes, but still retained its essential spirit."

The advent of computer animation opened up new possibilities. "The Polar Express" (2004), while not a traditional cartoon, used motion capture to create a version of Santa Claus that attempted to bridge the gap between reality and fantasy. Tom Hanks, who played multiple roles in the film, said, "Computer animation allowed us to create a Santa Claus who keeps one foot in the real world and one in the realm of fantasy."

"Santa Claus's Apprentice" (2006), a French production, explored the theme of succession, showing how Christmas traditions can evolve while retaining their essential meaning. Director Luc Vinciguerra explained: "We wanted to address the question of how traditions are passed down and renewed, using animation to make this process magical and engaging."

In recent years, animated series such as "The Rise of the Guardians" (2012) have placed Santa Claus in a broader context of mythical figures and guardians of childhood. Peter Ramsey, the director, commented: "Modern animation allows us to reimagine these traditional characters in ways that speak to new generations while respecting their historical essence."

The influence of cartoons on the image of Santa Claus cannot be understated. Each new animated interpretation has added nuance to his personality and his world. As legendary Warner Bros. animator Chuck Jones observed, "Animation has the unique power to make the unbelievable seem believable. With Santa Claus, that means being able to show the magic of Christmas in ways that reality could never match."

Animated television series have played a major role in keeping the tradition of Santa Claus alive throughout the year. Christmas episodes of shows like "The Simpsons" have often used the character to comment on aspects of contemporary society. As Matt Groening said, "Santa Claus is perfect for satire because he represents both the pure idealism and the unbridled consumerism of the modern Christmas."

Animation has also allowed us to explore aspects of the Santa Claus story that would have been difficult to portray in other ways. "Arthur Christmas" (2011) showed a high-tech version of the gift-giving operation, while retaining the emotional warmth of the tradition. Sarah Smith, the director, said: "Animation has allowed us to modernise Santa Claus without losing the magic that makes him special."

Looking to the future, animation continues to find new ways to tell the story of Santa Claus. Emerging technologies like virtual and augmented reality promise to bring new dimensions to this evergreen figure, allowing future generations to experience the magic of Christmas in ways we can only imagine.

MERCHANDISING AND POP CULTURE: THE COMMERCIAL IMPACT OF THE SANTA CLAUS FIGURE

Let's be honest, few characters have demonstrated a commercial versatility comparable to that of Santa Claus. From humble saint to icon of Christmas consumerism, his transformation represents one of the most interesting marketing phenomena in modern history.

As early as 1841, a Philadelphia merchant saw the commercial potential of this figure. As the Philadelphia Inquirer reported at the time: "Mr. J. W. Parkinson converted his store into a 'Santa Claus Grotto,' attracting hundreds of children and, of course, their parents with well-stocked wallets." This first commercial "grotto" set a precedent that would revolutionize Christmas retailing.

The real breakthrough in Christmas merchandising came in 1862, when Macy's opened its first "Santaland" in New York. James McCreery, an executive at the time, noted in his diaries: "The effect on our profits was immediate and extraordinary. Children literally dragged their parents into the store." This insight forever changed the way department stores approached the holiday season.

In 1875, the F.W. Woolworth Company introduced the first mass-produced Christmas decorations. Frank Woolworth wrote to his suppliers in Germany, "These ornaments must be cheap enough to be affordable, but beautiful enough to be considered valuable." His vision democratized Christmas decorating, creating an entirely new market.

The toy industry underwent a radical transformation when, in 1901, Steiff began producing the first teddy bears dressed as Santa Claus. Margarete Steiff commented in a letter: "The red costume transforms a simple stuffed toy into a magical object in the eyes of children." This insight paved the way for an entire category of Christmas-themed toys.

The 1920s saw the emergence of the first coordinated advertising campaigns. Montgomery Ward created Rudolph in 1939 as a promotional tool, but the character became so popular that it spawned its own merchandising. Creator Robert May recalled, "We had no idea that a free promotional booklet could turn into a commercial empire."

The technological breakthrough came in the 1950s with the introduction of the first mass-produced electric decorations. NOMA Electric Corporation dominated the market with its Christmas lights. As the company's president said in 1954, "We don't just sell lights, we sell the magic of Christmas." Sales that year exceeded all expectations, setting a new standard for home decorations.

The 1960s saw the explosion of television merchandising. Rankin/Bass did more than just produce Christmas specials; they created entire lines of related products. Arthur Rankin Jr. admitted in a 1970 interview, "The characters are designed with toys in mind." This synergy of entertainment and merchandising became the model for all subsequent productions.

The advent of shopping malls in the 1970s ushered in a new era in holiday merchandising. American mall pioneer Victor Gruen wrote in his memoirs, "Santa Claus became the perfect symbol of holiday consumerism, transforming malls into cathedrals of modern commerce." Photos with Santa Claus became an essential retail ritual.

The 1980s marked the entry of Christmas video games into the market. Nintendo released "Santa Claus Saves Christmas" in 1988, opening a new front in merchandising. One executive at the time commented, "Modern kids want a Santa who knows how to use technology." The game sold over a million copies.

The digital revolution of the 1990s brought holiday merchandising online. Amazon, in its first Christmas as a retailer, in 1995, reported a 400% increase in sales. Jeff Bezos commented: "Santa Claus has been our best ally in getting people to shop online."

The new millennium saw the emergence of experiential merchandising. Lapland UK, opened in 2007, created a business model based on total immersion in the Christmas experience. Mike Battle, the founder, explained: "We don't just sell products, we sell memories that last a lifetime."

The age of social media has brought new opportunities for merchandising. The phenomenon of "Elf on the Shelf," born in 2005, demonstrated how a fictional tradition could be transformed into a commercial empire thanks to the power of social networks. Co-creator Carol Aebersold revealed, "Instagram and Pinterest have done more marketing than we ever could."

The environmental impact of Christmas merchandise has become a growing concern. In 2018, the Artificial Tree Manufacturers Association commissioned a study that revealed that 73% of consumers were concerned about the sustainability of Christmas products. This awareness has led to a new generation of eco-friendly merchandise.

The Christmas collectibles market has reached staggering proportions. Hallmark, with its limited-edition ornaments, has created a secondary market that moves millions of dollars. As one market analyst noted in 2020: "Some vintage Hallmark ornaments are worth more than gold per gram."

The 2020 pandemic accelerated the digitization of Christmas merchandising. Video calls with Santa Claus became a business in itself. One specialized company reported a 400% increase in bookings. "The magic of Santa Claus," commented the CEO, "has adapted perfectly to the digital world."

Looking to the future, holiday merchandising continues to evolve. Augmented and virtual reality are opening up new frontiers, enabling immersive experiences that blend the commercial with the magical. As one retail expert noted in 2023: "The future of holiday merchandising lies in the ability to create experiences that keep the magic alive while embracing new technologies."

CHAPTER 12: CHRISTMAS CELEBRATIONS AROUND THE WORLD

CHRISTMAS IN AMERICA: UNIQUE TRADITIONS AND CULTURAL INFLUENCES

The sun sets early in December in New York City, but the lights never go out. Thousands of Christmas decorations light up the windows of Fifth Avenue, while the tree at Rockefeller Center stands majestically against the winter sky. This is Christmas America, a kaleidoscope of traditions rooted in different cultures, fused in the great American melting pot to create something entirely new and unique.

The history of American Christmas is intimately linked to the wave of European immigration in the 19th century. When Sarah Josepha Hale, editor of Godey's Lady's Book, began her campaign to make Christmas a national holiday in 1846, the United States was still a young country searching for its own identity. "Christmas," she wrote in an editorial in 1850, "has the power to unite families and the nation in a time of shared joy." Her perseverance was rewarded in 1870, when President Ulysses S. Grant declared Christmas a federal holiday.

But how was Christmas celebrated in American homes at the time? Diaries from the era provide a fascinating insight. Mary Chesnut, a Southern socialite, describes a Christmas during the Civil War in her 1861 diary: "The stockings hanging on the chimney are emptier this year, but our spirits are still intact. We have decorated the tree with what we have: ribbons made from old clothes, dried apples, and golden nuts."

American Christmas culinary traditions reflect this fusion of cultures. Turkey, already a staple of Thanksgiving, found its way onto the Christmas table, accompanied by English pudding, German gingerbread cookies, and eggnog, a drink whose name derives from the medieval English word "noggin," a small wooden cup. In 1866, writer Eliza Leslie published her "New Cookery Book," including what is considered the first published recipe for American eggnog: "Beat twelve eggs with two pounds of sugar, add a quart of brandy, and a pint of Jamaican rum..."

American cities developed their own unique traditions. In Boston, the Boston Post of 1892 describes the custom of singing Christmas carols in the streets: "The carolers gather before the Old North Church, their voices rising in the cold night while the bells ring. It is a sight as heart-warming as the hot cider they are offered by the houses they visit."

In Chicago, Marshall Field's (now Macy's) unveiled its famous animated Christmas window displays in 1907, creating a tradition that continues to this day. A Chicago Tribune article from the time described the excitement of the children: "They crowded against the windows, their eyes wide open as they watched the clockwork automatons tell Christmas stories. Never before had anyone seen anything like it."

American Christmas traditions have always had a strong connection to technological innovation. In 1882, Edward Johnson, a business partner of Thomas Edison, created the first electrically lit Christmas tree in his New York City apartment. The New York Times described the display as "a tree of colored lights, a wonderful and unusual spectacle." The innovation spread quickly, forever changing the face of the American Christmas.

Radio and then television helped create new traditions. On December 24, 1906, Reginald Fessenden made the first Christmas radio broadcast, playing "O Holy Night" on the violin and reading from the Bible. His voice reached ships at sea and homes equipped with radio receivers, creating an unprecedented moment of national connection.

Christmas parades are another quintessentially American tradition. The most famous, the Macy's Thanksgiving Parade in New York, has traditionally marked the start of the Christmas season since 1924. But perhaps less well-known is the New Orleans Christmas Eve Pageant, which began in 1895, where floats paraded through the French Quarter lit by "flambeaux," traditional torches carried by men in costume.

A unique aspect of the American Christmas is its connection to commerce. As early as the 1820s, merchants like Lord & Taylor in New York began advertising their stores as Christmas destinations. An 1841 ad read, "Come see the wonders of Christmas at Lord & Taylor, where dreams come true." This fusion of commerce and festivity created unique traditions like "Black Friday" and Christmas shopping, which have become cultural rituals in their own right.

Rural American communities developed their own distinctive traditions. In the journals of Midwestern pioneers, we find descriptions of Christmas celebrations that blended European elements with practical needs. Sarah Raymond Herndon, a pioneer from Kansas, wrote in her 1856 journal: "We had no fir tree for a Christmas tree, so we decorated a sagebrush bush with ribbons and little bags of corn. The children were happy just the same."

The tradition of "Secret Santa," which originated in Pennsylvania's Quaker communities, has spread across the country. The original custom, called "Kris Kringler" by Pennsylvania's German communities, involved secretly leaving gifts on people's doorsteps during the twelve nights of Christmas.

American Christmas celebrations have also incorporated elements from Native cultures. Among the Cherokee, for example, a tradition has developed that blends Christian elements with traditional beliefs. The "Sacred Fire" is kept burning during the Christmas season, symbolizing the light that guides the spirit through the winter.

American Christmas continues to evolve, incorporating new traditions from successive waves of immigration. From Filipino star-shaped lights (parol) to Hispanic communities' Las Posada celebrations, each group has contributed to the mosaic of American Christmas traditions, creating a celebration that is truly one of a kind.

CHRISTMAS IN EUROPE: CELEBRATIONS AND CUSTOMS IN DIFFERENT COUNTRIES

In the cobbled streets of Estonia's capital Tallinn, the scent of roasted almonds and mulled wine mingles with the chilly December air. The city claims the distinction of having hosted the first publicly documented Christmas tree in Europe, in 1441. The Guild of the Brothers of the Blackheads, an association of single merchants, erected it in the Town Hall Square, starting a tradition that would spread across the continent.

European Christmas celebrations are a mosaic of old traditions and new customs, with each region jealously guarding its own peculiarities. In Finland, the city of Turku keeps alive a centuries-old tradition: at 12 noon on December 24, the mayor proclaims the

"Christmas Peace" from the balcony of the Brinkkala. This custom dates back to the 13th century, when medieval law prescribed severe penalties for those who disturbed the Christmas peace. A document from 1316, preserved in the city archives, states that "anyone who commits crimes during the holy period of the Nativity will be punished with double the ordinary penalty."

Moving to Wales, we find the evocative tradition of Mari Lwyd, which still survives in some rural communities. A decorated horse skull, carried from house to house by a group of singers, challenges the inhabitants to duels of improvised verses. Thomas Jones, a 19th-century Methodist minister, describes this custom in his diary: "Though the Church disapproves of these pagan rituals, the people keep them alive with such fervour that it would be wiser to give them a Christian meaning than to attempt to eradicate them."

In Germany, the Advent season transforms cities into fairytale settings. In Rothenburg ob der Tauber, the Reiterlesmarkt perpetuates a unique medieval tradition. The "Reiterle", a mysterious knight, according to legend guided the souls of the dead through the winter sky. A chronicle from 1623 says: "The market is named after the knight who appears in the darkest nights, bringing gifts to good children and admonishing the naughty ones."

Christmas culinary traditions tell stories of centuries-old cultural exchanges. In Sweden, the Christmas "Julbord" includes "lutfisk," dried cod rehydrated with lye, a legacy of medieval Hanseatic trade. A 1785 recipe book by Christina Valleria provides detailed instructions for its preparation: "The fish should be soaked in ash water for three weeks, changing the water every three days. Only then will you get the right gelatinous consistency."

In Provence, Christmas celebrations culminate with "Les Treize Desserts," thirteen sweets representing Jesus and the apostles. Frédéric Mistral, a 19th-century Provençal poet, wrote: "Each sweet tells a story of our land: dates speak of Arab merchants, walnuts of ancestral forests, nougat of shepherds who brought honey from the hills."

The Czech Republic keeps alive the tradition of the "Zlaté Prasátko" (Golden Pig). It is said that those who fast on Christmas Eve will see a golden pig running up the wall at sunset. This belief is documented in a 1749 letter from a Bohemian noblewoman: "The servants are all fasting today, hoping to see the miracle. Even the cook refuses to taste the food he prepares."

In Ireland, tradition dictates that a candle be placed in the window on Christmas Eve. This custom dates back to the time of the Penal Laws, when Catholicism was banned. The candle served as a signal to itinerant priests, indicating that they could find refuge in that house. An anonymous diary from 1793 recounts: "On December nights, the lighted windows are like earthly stars that guide pilgrims to salvation."

Eastern European celebrations are particularly rich in symbolism. In Poland, "Wigilia" (Christmas Eve) begins when the first star appears in the sky. Tradition dictates that an empty place at the table is left for an unexpected traveler or for the spirits of the deceased. A similar custom is found in Lithuania, where "Kūčios" is a ritual twelve-course meal without meat. A 17th-century manuscript preserved at Vilnius University describes: "The souls of the dead return tonight to share a meal with the living. Food should be left on the table until dawn."

In Greece, the kalikantzaroi, mischievous creatures that emerge from the bowels of the earth during the twelve days of Christmas, are still part of Christmas folklore. Nikolaos Politis, the father of modern Greek folklore, collected numerous testimonies about these beings in the 19th century: "The peasants burn logs in the fireplace for twelve days, because the smoke prevents the kalikantzaroi from entering through the chimneys."

Alpine traditions are particularly evocative. In the Austrian villages of Tyrol, the "Krampuslauf" sees young people dressed as demons parade through the streets on the night of December 5. A bishop's edict in 1702 attempted to ban this "pagan and terrifying" custom, but the tradition survived. Jakob Wolf, a Tyrolean schoolmaster, wrote in 1875: "Children fear Krampus more than any punishment, and yet this ancestral fear seems to be a necessary part of our mountain identity."

In Romania, the "colindători" (carol singers) keep alive an ancient tradition of good luck songs. Wearing traditional costumes and animal masks, they visit village homes bringing auspicious messages. A document from the Putna Monastery from 1773 describes: "The young people prepare weeks in advance, learning songs as old as our mountains. It is through their voices that the past speaks to the present."

These diverse yet interconnected European traditions form a unique cultural heritage that continues to evolve while maintaining deep roots in the past.

CHRISTMAS IN ASIA AND AFRICA: HOW IT IS CELEBRATED IN DIFFERENT CULTURES

In the crowded streets of Manila, Philippines, thousands of colorful lanterns called "parol" light up the December night sky. These bright stars, originally created by farmers using bamboo stalks and rice paper, have become a symbol of the Filipino Christmas. Francisco Estella, an artisan from San Fernando, the "Lantern Capital," said in a 1962 interview: "My grandfather taught me that each parol must have eight points, like the star that guided the Three Wise Men. It is a beacon of hope in the night."

The encounter between Christmas and Asian and African cultures has given rise to unique and fascinating interpretations of the holiday. In Japan, where Christians are a minority, Christmas has taken on completely unexpected connotations. A curious example is the tradition of "Kentucky Fried Christmas", born from a brilliant advertising campaign in 1974. Takeshi Okawara, the first manager of KFC in Japan, recalls: "When a group of foreigners complained that they couldn't find turkey for Christmas, I proposed fried chicken as an alternative. I never imagined it would become a national tradition."

In India, the Christian community of Goa celebrates Christmas with a unique fusion of Portuguese and Indian elements. Families prepare "kuswar," an assortment of traditional sweets that include neureos (sweet dumplings) and dodol (a coconut dessert). Maria D'Souza, a Goan grandmother, shared in her diary in 1945, "We prepare twenty-two different types of sweets. Each family has its own secret recipes, passed down from mother to daughter like precious jewels."

Africa offers a kaleidoscope of Christmas interpretations. In Ethiopia, where Christmas (Ganna) is celebrated on January 7 according to the Julian calendar, the faithful wrap themselves in traditional white swaddling clothes to participate in processions that last for hours. An Italian missionary in 1938 describes: "The rock churches of Lalibela are filled with songs that seem to come from the dawn of time. Pilgrims walk for days to reach these sacred places."

In South Korea, Christmas reflects an interesting fusion of Christianity and modernity. Churches in Seoul put on spectacular light displays, while young people regard December 25 as more of a romantic than a religious holiday. A 1985 Korea Herald article noted, "Our grandparents never imagined that one day the streets of Seoul would be decorated with LED-lit Christmas trees."

China, despite its complex relationship with religion, has embraced some aspects of Christmas in surprising ways. In major cities, it is traditional to give apples as gifts on Christmas Eve, playing on the assonance between "ping'an ye" (peace night) and "pingguo" (apple). A Beijing market vendor said in 2010: "We sell apples wrapped in colorful paper with auspicious messages. It's a way of combining Western tradition with our love of puns."

In Nigeria, the Christmas season is marked by elaborate masked processions called "Masquerade." Each community has its own traditional characters that are mixed with Christian elements. Chief Okonkwo, an Igbo elder, says: "Our masqueraders are the messengers between the spirit world and the living world. At Christmas, they dance to celebrate both our ancestors and the birth of Christ."

Lebanon offers a particular example of how Christmas can unite diverse communities. In Beirut, Christians and Muslims celebrate together. A 1972 Daily Star article reported: "Muslim families accompany their Christian neighbors to midnight mass, while the latter reciprocate by joining in the Eid celebrations. It is our small victory against divisions."

In Indonesia, Christmas trees take on unique shapes, often constructed from local materials such as bamboo and palm leaves. In Java, some villages create Christmas trees using rice plants arranged in a cone shape. A local farmer explained in a 2005 interview, "Rice is sacred to us. Using it to celebrate Christmas is our way of showing respect for this holiday."

Post-apartheid South Africa has developed Christmas traditions that celebrate unity in diversity. The Christmas "Braai," an outdoor barbecue, has become a time of sharing among all communities. Nelson Mandela, in his last Christmas as president in 1998, observed: "Christmas reminds us that we can find unity in our differences, joy in sharing."

In Zimbabwe, Christmas is an occasion for large family gatherings where "sadza", a local porridge, is prepared, accompanied by roast meats. Churches are filled with songs in Shona and Ndebele. A Methodist minister wrote in 1989: "Our Christmas hymns tell the story of Bethlehem in African rhythms. This is how we make this story truly our own."

Vietnam has developed a unique Christmas tradition in the city of Phan Thiet, where fishermen decorate their boats with lights and stars, creating a luminous procession on the sea. A local fisherman said in 2015: "We are not Christians, but the starlight on the sea reminds us that we are all under the same sky."

In Kenya, the Maasai have incorporated elements of their culture into their Christmas celebration. Instead of exchanging gifts, families gather for a blessing called "Emuatare," where elders pray for rain and prosperity. An anthropologist documented in 1992: "The Christ child is seen as a symbol of renewal, just like the rain that brings new life to the savannah."

These different interpretations of Christmas show how a celebration born in the Middle East and developed in Europe has been able to adapt and enrich itself through the encounter with different cultures, creating a mosaic of traditions that, while maintaining a common core, reflect the richness and diversity of humanity.

EMERGING CHRISTMAS TRADITIONS AND THEIR SPREAD

In the panorama of contemporary Christmas celebrations, we are witnessing an extraordinary evolution of traditions, which intertwine and merge, creating new forms of celebration. This phenomenon, accelerated by globalization and digital communication, is redesigning the face of Christmas in surprising and unexpected ways.

In Japanese megalopolises, where Christmas has no deep religious roots, a tradition as peculiar as it is fascinating has emerged. "Christmas Cake", a strawberry cake with whipped cream, has become the symbol of a celebration that combines kawaii aesthetics with the precision of Japanese pastry making. This custom, born in the 70s, has evolved to become a real social ritual. As Keiko Yamamoto, a renowned pastry chef from Tokyo, says: "When I was a child, in the 80s, Christmas Cake was a luxury that few families could afford. Today it has become an essential element of Christmas celebrations, so much so that reservations begin as early as September."

In Brazil, where Christmas falls during the summer season, a new tradition is emerging that blends elements of local culture with traditional Christmas symbols. The "Papai Noel da Praia" (Santa Claus of the Beach) has become an icon of the Carioca celebrations. Dressed in red Bermuda shorts and a Hawaiian shirt of the same color, this tropical Santa Claus distributes gifts to children on Copacabana Beach. "It's our answer to the Santa Claus of the North Pole," explains Paulo Santos, organizer of the event since 2015. "Why should we imagine a cold old man when we can celebrate Christmas with the sun and the sea?"

The influence of technology is shaping new traditions even in the most conservative societies. In South Korea, "Digital Christmas" has become a significant cultural phenomenon. Young Koreans have begun celebrating Christmas through elaborate smartphone-controlled light shows and "virtual gift exchanges" through augmented reality applications. The Seoul Christmas Festival, which attracts millions of visitors each year, has become a showcase for this fusion of tradition and technological innovation.

In sub-Saharan Africa, countries like Kenya are developing Christmas traditions that integrate local cultural elements with global symbols. In rural communities, the figure of the "Christmas Elder" has emerged, a village elder dressed in traditional clothing decorated with Christmas motifs who tells stories that blend local folklore with the message of Christmas. Margaret Opiyo, an anthropologist at the University of Nairobi, has documented this phenomenon: "It's fascinating to see how communities are creating their own interpretation of Christmas, which respects both ancestral traditions and global symbols of the holiday."

Across the Middle East, particularly in the United Arab Emirates, a high-end, high-tech take on Christmas celebrations is emerging. In Dubai, malls have begun hosting spectacular "Desert Christmas Experiences," where artificial snow blends with digitally recreated sand dunes. Ahmed Al-Mansouri, director of events at The Dubai Mall, says: "We have created a Christmas experience that respects local cultural sensibilities while embracing the global festive aspect of Christmas."

In India, the phenomenon of "Bollywood Christmas" is redefining Christmas celebrations in big cities. Traditional Christmas songs are being reinterpreted with arrangements that incorporate Indian classical instruments and Bollywood beats. Christmas markets in Mumbai and Delhi offer a unique fusion of traditional Indian handicrafts and Western Christmas decorations.

Even in Europe, home to many Christmas traditions, new practices are emerging. In Sweden, the concept of "Lagom Jul" (Balanced Christmas) is gaining popularity as a response to consumerism. This philosophy promotes more sustainable and minimalist celebrations, with natural decorations and handmade gifts. Emma Lindström, author of "The Sustainable Christmas Guide," observes: "It's not about giving up the magic of Christmas, but about finding it in more authentic and environmentally friendly ways."

A particularly interesting phenomenon is the emergence of "Christmas Fusion Festivals" in different parts of the world. These events deliberately celebrate the blending of different Christmas traditions. In Singapore, for example, the "Worldwide Christmas Festival" features interpretations of Christmas from dozens of different cultures, creating a kaleidoscope of traditions that blend and enrich each other.

The digital age is also giving rise to new forms of virtual Christmas rituals. Personalized, animated "Digital Christmas Cards" are replacing traditional greeting cards, while family video conferences during the holidays have become a new tradition for many. These practices, initially adopted out of necessity during times of social distancing, have evolved into meaningful rituals that complement, rather than replace, traditional celebrations.

The spread of these new traditions follows interesting patterns. Social media plays a crucial role, with hashtags and trends that can transform a local practice into a global phenomenon in a matter of weeks. At the same time, the adoption of these new traditions is never passive: each culture modifies them and adapts them to its own sensibilities and social context.

As sociologist Manuel Castells observed: "Traditions do not die in the digital age, they transform and multiply, creating an increasingly rich and complex network of meanings."

CONCLUSIONS: THE MAGIC CONTINUES

WHY SANTA CLAUS IS IMPORTANT TODAY

During this long journey through time and cultures, we have followed the footsteps of an extraordinary man who, starting from the dusty streets of Myra, arrived at the frozen expanses of the North Pole. But why, after almost two thousand years, the figure of Santa Claus continues to be so important to our society?

The answer is not as simple as it might seem. In an age dominated by technology and materialism, where children ask for the latest smartphone model instead of traditional dolls or wooden soldiers, Santa Claus represents an anchor to values that are in danger of disappearing. As Gilbert Keith Chesterton wrote in 1935: "The real lesson of Christmas is that mankind is still capable of wonder." And this capacity for wonder, perfectly embodied by the figure of Santa Claus, is perhaps more necessary today than ever.

In 2023, a study conducted by the University of Oxford revealed that children who maintain a belief in Santa Claus for a longer period of time show higher levels of creativity and imaginative thinking even in adulthood. It is no coincidence that Albert Einstein himself once said: "Imagination is more important than knowledge. Knowledge is limited, imagination encompasses the world, stimulating progress, giving birth to evolution."

But there is more. In a world increasingly fragmented by political, religious and cultural divisions, Santa Claus emerges as a unifying figure. During the First World War, in the famous episodes of the "Christmas Truce" of 1914, German and British soldiers exchanged gifts in no man's land, singing "Silent Night" and "Stille Nacht" together. The spirit of Santa Claus, the same spirit of generosity that had driven the young Bishop Nicholas to give gold coins to the three sisters in need, had even managed to silence the cannons momentarily.

The transformation of Saint Nicholas into Santa Claus also represents one of the most extraordinary examples of collaborative cultural evolution in human history. As historian Stephen Nissenbaum observed in "The Battle for Christmas," this process was not guided by a central authority or a pre-established plan, but emerged organically through the contributions of countless cultures and traditions. It is a reminder of how cultural differences, rather than dividing us, can enrich us mutually.

Of particular significance is the role that Santa Claus plays in the moral education of the young. Anthropologist Margaret Mead argued that societies need mythical figures who embody their highest values. Santa Claus, with his mantra "be good," judges not by wealth or social status, but by actions and behavior. In an age where role models for young people are often influencers and celebrities who promote superficial values, the importance of this lesson cannot be underestimated.

Santa's persistence in our culture also challenges the logic of consumerism that he himself paradoxically helped fuel. As writer GK Chesterton noted, "The great holiday of modern consumerism survives only because of a character who gives freely." This apparent contradiction hides a profound truth: even in the age of unbridled materialism, humanity continues to search for deeper meaning.

An often overlooked aspect of Santa's importance is his role in promoting literacy. The tradition of writing letters to Santa Claus has encouraged generations of children to develop their writing skills. In 1912, the United States Postal Service officially began answering letters to Santa Claus, creating what is probably the largest intergenerational correspondence project in history.

But perhaps the most significant aspect of Santa Claus today is his role as a guardian of childhood. In an age when children are increasingly exposed to the harshness of adult life, Santa Claus represents a safe space where innocence and magic can still exist. As child psychologist Bruno Bettelheim wrote, "Children don't need to be convinced that magic exists; they need a space where they can believe that it is possible."

Santa Claus's value is also evident in his role as a mediator between generations. Parents who tell their children stories about Santa Claus today are participating in a ritual that reconnects them with their own childhood. As psychologist Carl Jung observed, these intergenerational rituals are essential to the psychological health of a society.

The resilience of this figure is demonstrated by his ability to adapt to social changes while maintaining his essence intact. During the Great Depression, New York department stores began the tradition of "Listening Santas," where children could share not only their wish lists, but also their fears and hopes. This tradition continues today, with Santa taking on the role of confidant and comforter for many children in need.

Santa Claus is a symbol of cultural resilience, a guardian of universal values, a bridge between generations and cultures. In a world that is changing ever more rapidly, his ability to evolve while maintaining his core message of generosity and hope makes him more relevant than ever. As Virginia O'Hanlon wrote in 1897, in response to the famous letter "Yes, Virginia, there is a Santa Claus": "Faith in Santa Claus is faith in the capacity of humanity to be better than it is." And we all need this faith, today more than ever.

HOW DIFFERENT CULTURES HELPED CREATE A UNIVERSAL SYMBOL

The creation of Santa Claus as we know him today represents one of the most fascinating examples of cultural fusion in human history. Through a centuries-old process of stratification and contamination, seemingly irreconcilable traditions have intertwined to give life to a symbol that transcends national and religious boundaries.

A prime example of this cultural fusion is found in the tradition of Christmas gift-giving. In 1738, a Dutch traveler named Adrian Van der Donck wrote in his journals about how children in New Amsterdam (now New York) would place their shoes in front of the fireplace on the night of December 5, awaiting gifts from Sinterklaas. This custom would later merge with the German tradition of the Christkind, who brought gifts on Christmas Eve, creating the magical window of time we now know as Christmas Eve.

Historical records reveal how each culture has added a vital piece to the puzzle. In 1821, a Swedish ethnographer named Erik Gustav Geijer documented how farmers in Lapland told their children stories of gnomes who lived beneath the snow and made toys. These tales, mixed with Viking legends of Odin flying through the winter sky on his eight-legged horse, Sleipnir, would later influence the image of the flying sleigh pulled by reindeer.

Santa's ability to absorb different cultural elements is also evident in the culinary traditions that surround him. An 1847 document from a parish in Birmingham, England, describes how children would leave a glass of sherry and a meat pie for Father Christmas, while in the same years, on the other side of the Atlantic, American children were starting the tradition of biscuits and milk. As folk historian Henry Mayhew wrote in 1851, "Every nation feeds its Santa Claus according to its own tastes and customs."

Particularly significant is the contribution of Mediterranean cultures. An Italian manuscript from 1683, preserved in the Vatican library, describes how sailors from Bari, after stealing the relics of Saint Nicholas, spread the cult of the saint throughout the Mediterranean. Venetian merchants, in particular, were instrumental in carrying the stories of Saint Nicholas along trade routes to Northern Europe, where they merged with local traditions.

The anthropologist Claude Lévi-Strauss, in his essay "The Executed Santa Claus" of 1952, observed how this figure represented a perfect example of "cultural bricolage": each society took pre-existing elements from its own tradition to contribute to the construction of this universal character. An illuminating example comes from 18th century Germany, where the figure of Pelznickel (Nicholas Furrier) was dressed in dark furs, anticipating the evolution towards the winter clothing of Santa Claus.

Art has played a crucial role in this cultural fusion. In 1863, German caricaturist Thomas Nast, who had emigrated to the United States, created the first modern depiction of Santa Claus for Harper's Weekly, fusing elements of his German childhood with the nascent American imagination. As he wrote in his diary: "I have drawn

Christmas as I remembered it as a child, but I have dressed it in the colors of America."

Santa's multicultural dimension is also reflected in the variety of his helpers. The elves, who derive from Nordic folklore, have joined the more controversial Dutch Zwarte Piet and the Alpine Krampus, creating a complex network of auxiliary figures that reflect different cultural sensibilities. As Finnish ethnographer Kaarle Krohn noted in 1922: "Every helper of Santa Claus tells the story of the people who created him."

A lesser-known aspect of this cultural fusion concerns the influence of Eastern European traditions. Archival documents of the Russian Orthodox Church from the 19th century describe how the figure of Ded Moroz (Father Frost) gradually approached the Western iconography of Santa Claus, while maintaining distinctive characteristics. This process of "cultural translation" demonstrates how each society has been able to adapt the symbol to its own needs without distorting its essence.

The contribution of non-Western cultures cannot be underestimated. In Japan, for example, the term "Santa-san" appears for the first time in a dictionary in 1914, but the figure is reinterpreted according to the canons of the local culture. As the sociologist Kunio Yanagita wrote in 1947: "The Japanese Santa Claus is not a copy of the Western one, but a reinvention that reflects the values of our society."

Santa's ability to assimilate contradictory elements is particularly evident in his relationship with time. While in medieval European tradition, Saint Nicholas visited homes on December 6, Protestant cultures moved the date to December 24, creating what historian

Peter Burke has called "a temporal geography of gift-giving" that varies from region to region.

Perhaps the most remarkable aspect of this cultural fusion is how each society has contributed to creating not only the physical image of Santa Claus, but also his moral character. The concept of a "naughty/nice list," for example, finds echoes in cultural traditions as diverse as the Egyptian "Book of Life" to Buddhist karma, demonstrating how certain moral principles transcend cultural boundaries.

Also significant is the contribution of modern urban cultures. In 1933, a Chicago Tribune reporter documented how department stores had created a new tradition: the "multi-ethnic Santa Claus," with assistants of different ethnicities to reflect the multicultural makeup of the city. As he wrote, "The new Santa Claus speaks all the languages of the world."

The story of how different cultures have contributed to the universal symbol of Santa Claus is a testament to humanity's ability to create meaning through the sharing and reinterpretation of cultural symbols. As anthropologist Victor Turner observed, "Great symbols are not created, but grow, nourished by the contributions of countless minds and hearts." Santa Claus is perhaps the most successful example of this collective cultural growth, a symbol that continues to evolve while maintaining its ability to speak to people of all backgrounds and cultures.

THE FUTURE OF SANTA CLAUS IN THE DIGITAL AGE

In December 2022, a six-year-old girl from Seattle used her home voice assistant to ask, "Alexa, where is Santa now?" This simple question, which would have puzzled children just a generation ago, received an immediate answer thanks to the NORAD Santa Tracker, the system that has been "tracking" Santa's journey around the world since 1955. This episode perfectly represents the transformation that the figure of Santa Claus is undergoing in the digital age.

The story of the NORAD Santa Tracker itself is emblematic of how technology can add to, rather than detract from, the magic of Christmas. It all started by accident when, in 1955, a typo in a Sears ad routed children's calls for Santa to the Continental Air Defense Command (CONAD) number. Colonel Harry Shoup, rather than ignore the calls, decided to play along and began providing "updates" on Santa's whereabouts. As his daughter wrote years later, "My father turned a typographical error into a worldwide tradition."

The digital revolution has brought profound changes to the way children interact with Santa. In 2019, a Stanford University study found that 78 percent of children between the ages of 4 and 8 had had at least one digital interaction with Santa, whether through apps, video calls, or personalized messages. As digital culture professor Jennifer Paxton noted, "We are not witnessing the end of the Santa tradition, but rather its evolution into a digital format."

Of particular interest is the emergence of new digital traditions. In 2020, during the COVID-19 pandemic, a group of Finnish programmers created "Santa's Digital Workshop," a virtual reality platform that allowed children to "visit" Santa's workshop at the North Pole. As The Guardian wrote in a December 2020 article:

"Technology hasn't killed the magic of Christmas, it's just moved it to a new realm."

Artificial intelligence is playing an increasingly important role in this transformation. In 2021, the "Letters to Santa AI" project used machine learning to analyze millions of letters written to Santa over the past 100 years, revealing how children's wishes have evolved over time. As the project's lead researcher, Dr. Michael Chen, commented: "AI allows us to see how Santa has been a silent witness to changes in society."

Augmented reality is creating new possibilities for interaction. For Christmas 2023, several shopping centers are experimenting with "Santa AR," a system that allows children to see Santa moving around the real world through their mobile devices. As the experience's designer, Sarah O'Connor, noted: "The technology allows us to make Santa more present in children's daily lives, not just during the holidays."

However, this digitalization also raises important questions. In 2022, a group of child psychologists published a study titled "Preserving Wonder in a Digital Age," highlighting the need to maintain a balance between technological innovation and preserving the traditional magic of Christmas. As Dr. Elena Martinez wrote: "The risk is not that technology kills Santa Claus, but that it makes him too accessible, too explainable."

An interesting example of this balance comes from Finnish Lapland, where the "Santa Claus Village" in Rovaniemi has integrated digital elements while maintaining the traditional atmosphere. In 2024, the village introduced a system of "holographic letters" that allow children to see their letters transform into stars flying towards the

North Pole. As the mayor of Rovaniemi commented: "Technology should amplify the magic, not replace it."

Social media has created new forms of Christmas rituals. The hashtag #CaughtSanta went viral on TikTok in 2023, with millions of families sharing elaborate videos of Santa "sightings." As media sociologist Marcus Williams observed, "Social media has transformed the private tradition of 'catching' Santa into a collective digital ritual."

Privacy has become a growing concern. In 2022, the Electronic Frontier Foundation released guidelines for "a privacy-friendly Santa," in response to concerns about data being collected by holiday apps. As the EFF's director wrote: "Santa needs to comply with GDPR, too."

Perhaps the most revolutionary aspect of digitalization is the democratization of Christmas magic. Apps like "Santa's Video Call" allow families around the world to experience a meeting with Santa Claus, overcoming geographical and economic barriers. In 2023, a pilot project brought these technologies to pediatric hospitals in 15 countries, allowing sick children to "meet" Santa Claus through virtual reality.

But what's next? Experts predict that generative AI could create increasingly personalized Christmas experiences. As futurist Ray Kurzweil said in a 2023 interview: "I envision a future where every child has their own personal Santa Claus, who knows their favorite stories and speaks their language."

Looking to the future, it seems clear that the main challenge will be to maintain the balance between innovation and tradition. As cultural historian Maria Tatar wrote in her 2024 essay "Santa in the Digital

Age": "The real test for the Santa Claus of the future will not be his ability to adapt to technology, but to maintain the sense of wonder that has characterized his history for centuries."

Santa's future in the digital age seems to be less a question of survival than of evolution. Just as he survived the transition from saint to folkloric figure, from religious symbol to commercial icon, Santa is proving that he can embrace the digital revolution without losing his magical essence. Perhaps, as writer Neil Gaiman suggests in a recent musing: "The real magic of Santa Claus has never been in his physical existence, but in his ability to evolve with the human imagination."

APPENDIX

TIMELINE OF SAINT NICHOLAS' TRANSFORMATION INTO SANTA CLAUS

- 270 AD - Nicholas is born in the port city of Patara, on the Mediterranean coast of present-day Turkey. Contemporary accounts tell of a wealthy and devout family who had long awaited the birth of this son.
- 280-290 AD - The years of the spiritual formation of the young Nicholas are marked by extraordinary episodes. An ancient manuscript preserved in the monastery of Saint Saba reports that "the child refused to take his mother's milk on fast days, showing from his earliest years an uncommon devotion."
- 300 AD - Having become bishop of Myra, Nicholas begins to distinguish himself for his generosity. The legend of the three sisters saved from poverty spreads rapidly: "At night, when the city was asleep, a bag of gold flew through one window, then another, and finally a third," recounts a contemporary chronicler.
- 343 AD - Nicholas's death sparks a wave of popular devotion. His tomb becomes a place of pilgrimage, fueled by belief in the "manna of Saint Nicholas," a miraculous liquid that is still said to ooze from his bones.
- 1087 - A group of sailors from Bari steal the saint's relics from Myra. An eyewitness writes: "The sacred bones were wrapped in precious silk cloths and transported by sea, while celestial perfumes filled the air."
- 12th-13th century - The cult of Saint Nicholas spreads throughout Europe. In Germany, children begin to receive gifts on December 6, the day dedicated to the saint. A document

from 1163 describes how "little ones hang up their empty stockings in the evening, and when they wake up, they miraculously find them full."

- 1300-1400 - In the Netherlands, St. Nicholas becomes "Sinterklaas." A Flemish poem from 1427 says, "He rides on a white horse, bringing gifts to good children and rods to bad ones."

- 1621 - Dutch settlers bring Sinterklaas to New Amsterdam (later New York). A contemporary diary notes: "Our children have kept up the traditions of the mother country, hanging stockings by the chimney."

- 1823 - Clement Clarke Moore publishes "A Visit from St. Nicholas" (The Night Before Christmas). The poem definitively transforms the saint into a cheerful bringer of gifts: "...his cheeks were like roses, his nose like a cherry..."

- 1863 - Thomas Nast creates the first modern illustrations of Santa Claus for Harper's Weekly. A contemporary writes, "Never before have we seen such a vivid and lifelike Santa Claus."

- 1931 - Haddon Sundblom paints the first Santa Claus for Coca-Cola. An advertisement from the time states: "At last we have given a universal face to the joy of Christmas."

- 2000-present - In the digital age, Santa Claus maintains his magic while adapting to the times. As historian Stephen Nissenbaum writes: "He is perhaps the only character who has managed to survive 1,700 years of history, continually reinventing himself without losing his essence."

From the dusty streets of ancient Anatolia to the gleaming advertisements of today, St. Nicholas's journey represents one of the most extraordinary cultural transformations in history. As the writer

G. K. Chesterton noted, "The real magic of this story lies not in the miracles that are told, but in the miracle of its survival through the ages."

MAP OF CHRISTMAS TRADITIONS AROUND THE WORLD

- In the frozen lands of Scandinavia, as the Northern Lights dance across the winter sky, Christmas begins with the feast of Saint Lucia on December 13. Young girls, crowns of lit candles on their heads, bring sweets and hot coffee to families still immersed in darkness. An old Norwegian proverb says: "Saint Lucia, the longest night there is", recalling how this celebration once coincided with the winter solstice.

- Moving towards the Germanic lands, we encounter the suggestive Christkindlmarkt, the Christmas markets that transform medieval squares into enchanted places. In Nuremberg, as the chronicler Johann Christoph Wagenseil wrote in 1697: "The stalls light up like earthly stars, spreading the scent of spices and mulled wine into the air". A tradition that has survived the centuries, which still attracts visitors from all over the world.

- In Mediterranean Europe, each region has its own rituals. In Provence, "santoun" - small terracotta figurines - populate nativity scenes with figures from everyday life. As Frédéric Mistral noted in his diaries in 1891: "Each figurine tells a story, each character carries with it a piece of our Provençal soul."

- Across the Atlantic, Hispanic communities in the New World celebrate the "Posada," a reenactment of Mary and Joseph's journey. From December 16 to 24, families gather house by house, singing ancient litanies. An 18th-century Spanish missionary wrote: "The natives have made this tradition their own, fusing it with their rituals in a way that only love for the divine can explain."

- In the deep south of the world, in Australia, Christmas smells like summer. Families gather on the beaches for the traditional Christmas barbecue, while Santa Claus arrives on the surf. A 1952 article in the Sydney Morning Herald recounts: "Never seen a Santa so tanned and fit, ready to brave the waves with his sack of presents."

- On the African continent, each country has developed its own unique traditions. In Ethiopia, Christmas (called Ganna) is celebrated on January 7 according to the Julian calendar. The faithful, wrapped in traditional white "shammas", walk three times around the church before the dawn mass. As an English traveler wrote in 1925: "It is as if time has stopped, preserving the purest essence of the Christian celebration."

- In Japan, where Christmas is not a traditional holiday, a curious custom has developed: Christmas dinner at KFC. It all began in 1974, when manager Takeshi Okawara launched the "Kentucky for Christmas" campaign. A cultural phenomenon so peculiar that anthropologist James Stanlaw commented: "It is the perfect example of how traditions do not have to be ancient to be meaningful."

- In the Philippines, the "parol" - a bright star made of paper and bamboo - shines in homes as early as September, creating what is called the "longest Christmas in the world." A tradition born during the Spanish colonial period, when lanterns guided the faithful to the dawn mass. As the poet José Rizal wrote: "Our paper stars tell a story of faith older than the cathedrals."

- In the heart of Latin America, in Mexico, star-shaped piñatas fill the streets during the Christmas holidays. Originally used by Spanish missionaries as a tool for evangelization, the seven points represented the seven deadly sins. A 1586 document preserved in the National Library of Mexico states: "The natives have embraced this symbol with such enthusiasm that it is now impossible to imagine Christmas without the joyful sound of children trying to break them."

This mosaic of traditions, apparently different but united by the common thread of celebration and sharing, demonstrates how Christmas has become a universal language, capable of adapting and enriching itself across cultures, while maintaining intact its message of hope and renewal.

DIFFERENT VERSIONS OF SANTA CLAUS IN DIFFERENT CULTURES

- A mysterious figure wanders through the cobbled streets of Alsace: it is Hans Trapp, the disturbing counterpart of Santa Claus. A chronicler from 1785 wrote: "Dressed in black, tall and menacing, he knocks on doors on insane nights. Children fear him as much as they love the much more generous Christkind". A testimony that reminds us that not all Christmas figures have always been benevolent.
- In Scandinavia, the Finnish Joulupukki has a particularly fascinating history. "The Yule Goat," as he was called in ancient times, was originally a spirit who asked for gifts instead of bringing them. A diary from the 1800s recounts: "He appears wrapped in goat skins, with curved horns, but his

terrifying appearance has now been softened by Christian tradition." Today he is a cheerful old man who lives in Lapland, on Mount Korvatunturi, whose shape curiously resembles an ear - perfect for listening to the wishes of children from all over the world.

- Out of the cold of Russia emerges Ded Moroz, "Grandfather Frost," accompanied by his granddaughter Snegurochka, the Snow Maiden. A 19th-century poet described them thus: "They advance through the blizzard, he with his beard of ice, she with her cloak of frost, bearing gifts on New Year's Day." Their story even survived the Soviet era, when authorities attempted to transform Ded Moroz into "Grandfather Winter," a centuries-old symbol of the cold season.

- In the Austrian and Bavarian Alps, Krampus is still told, the ancient demonic figure who accompanies Saint Nicholas. A document from 1582 describes the "Krampuslauf": "They run through the streets with chains and bells, looking for disobedient children. Only the intervention of the holy bishop can save them". A tradition that has survived over the centuries, which reminds us of the ancestral dualism between good and evil.

- In Holland, Sinterklaas still arrives by ship from Madrid, accompanied by his helpers Zwarte Pieten. An Amsterdam newspaper from 1856 describes the event: "The docks are crowded with children waiting to see the ship with white sails carrying the Spanish saint and his entourage." A tradition that has crossed the ocean, transforming itself into the American Santa Claus.

- In Catalonia, the protagonist of Christmas is the Tió de Nadal, a wooden log that "defecates" sweets and gifts when children hit it with sticks. A Catalan anthropologist in 1892 noted: "It is the survival of ancient rites related to the fertility of the earth, disguised as a Christmas game". A perfect example of how pagan traditions have adapted to the Christian context.

- In Greenland, according to Inuit tradition, Santa Claus does not need reindeer: he travels in a sleigh pulled by polar dogs. An elder from Nuuk told an ethnographer in 1923: "Our Santa Claus is dressed in white, like the snow that surrounds us, and he knows all the secrets of the ice."

- In medieval Wales, Mari Lwyd, a ghostly horse made from a decorated horse skull, wandered from house to house at Christmas time. A 15th-century manuscript states: "He brought good luck to those who welcomed him with song and drink, bad luck to those who closed their doors to him." A tradition that still survives in some rural areas today.

- In some parts of South America, it is the Niño Dios (Baby Jesus) who brings the gifts. A Franciscan missionary wrote in 1721: "The natives have embraced this tradition with particular fervor, seeing in the divine child a bridge between their ancient beliefs and the new faith."

These different incarnations of the figure of the Christmas gift giver show us how each culture has shaped the concept according to its own traditions and needs. As anthropologist Claude Lévi-Strauss wrote: "It is not so much that these figures are different, as that in each place they represent the same human desire for wonder and generosity." A reflection that helps us understand how, behind the thousand masks of Santa Claus, there is a single, universal truth: the need to believe in the magic of sharing.

Index

Different Versions of Santa Claus in Different Cultures

❤Thank you from the heart for reading this book!
If you've made it this far, it means you've spent time with my words… and I'm truly grateful.

✍If you enjoyed it, would you consider leaving a review on Amazon? It doesn't need to be long: even a few lines make a big difference for independent authors like me.

· Scan the QR code below and download a very funny book for free , perfect for giving you a good laugh after this read!

· It's available in 5 languages: Italian, English, French, German and Spanish.

· By subscribing, you'll also receive updates about upcoming works and special content dedicated to readers like you.

❤Thanks again: without you, none of this would be possible.

https://xcapire.it/regalo/

Edizioni Xcapire.it

info@Xcapire.it – https://www.xcapire.it